MAKING LOVE WORK

A Radical Approach

A reconsideration of the personal and political
implications of a belief in the fundamentally
loving nature of human beings

MAKING LOVE WORK
A Radical Approach

by
John Button

TURNSTONE PRESS
Wellingborough, Northamptonshire

First published 1985

British Library Cataloguing in Publication Data

Button, John
  Making love work.
  1. Love
  I. Title
  248.4   BV4639

ISBN 0-85500-206-9

*Turnstone Press is part of
the Thorsons Publishing Group*

Printed and bound in Great Britain

Threats of war loom like an ice age,
Warning we must live as one,
And the walls we build against the cold
Are also walls against the sun,
And the glacier reaches everyone.
Time is short, but it's not too late,
What I want to know is: how does the world
    remain so preoccupied with hate?
And it's need versus greed,
And there are so many mouths to feed:
We must make the time for love,
Break the ground and plant the seed.
I want to be where children still laugh and dance and sing;
While you entrench against the winter
I will plant to save the spring.

from *The First Winds of Autumn*
a song by Jim Scott

Contents

Acknowledgements

Learning to love is a lifelong experience, and everybody I have ever loved or who has loved me should be acknowledged in the preparation of *Making Love Work*. A few people deserve special mention, though: David Young at Thorsons for asking me to write the book; Jan, Yves, Susanne, Helmut, Doro, Annie, Tina and Gabrielle for believing in my workshop technique; Joan and David for continuing to love me after thirty-five years; Gail and Jane for the hilarious meal when we invented the workshop personnel; Margaret for sustained support as writer to writer and one of my oldest friends; Ellie, Tess and Molly for space to type the manuscript; Calum and Kate for being there when I needed them; Catherine and Rosalind for being perfect models of unrestrained loving.

Laurieston,
March 1984

Introduction

This book is about loving and being loved. It is about love as it affects our everyday lives, and derives from the experience of my own life and of leading workshops on love. It is not intended to be a philosophical, theological or psychological treatise on the nature of love; far better qualified people than me have filled many volumes doing that job. I have, however, questioned many of the assumptions that we in our culture learn to make about love, and this is my justification in calling it a radical approach. To an extent, I have written the book in response to the people who have been in my workshops and who have suggested that a book on the theme of the workshops would be useful; to all those lovable people my thanks both for the suggestion and for many of the insights that have gone into *Making Love Work*.

There seem to be enormous problems when it comes to thinking about love; it's probably the most important and difficult concept that anyone can try to bend their brain round. Many people don't appear to think about the potential of love at all, they are more concerned with the problems that arise from an apparent lack of love. I can understand this to an extent. It seems useless to be idealistic when the world is so very far from being an ideal place. Yes, it would be wonderful if people all loved each other, but they obviously don't, so why bother messing around with romantic platitudes when there's so much real work to be done? And would it really be so wonderful if everybody loved each other all the time? Do we want to sit around on pink cushions gazing lovingly into one another's eyes, listening to Mantovani and reading the occasional passage of Patience Strong?

As for a political perspective on love, it hardly exists. Until recently many people who considered themselves to be politically aware gave little thought to it: Barbara Cartland, marriage and the church seemed to have maintained a possessive partnership in the reactionary commodity market of love. All highly suspect; nothing to do with changing the world.

But perversely, love won't go away. All that has resulted from an attempt to keep love out of public life is that a split has occurred in many people's lives between their active outside world where love seems to be irrelevant, and their private emotional existence where love continues to be vitally important. Love plays the same role in political activism as it has played in public life for centuries. It isn't acknowledged as having any importance, yet it keeps elbowing its way in, or at least the effects of lack of love do. It won't go away.

We must include love in a political analysis of personal and social change. But where to begin?

It's been a long exploration for me, and maybe if I tell you about some of the strands in my exploration it will help you to understand my current thinking.

A very important strand has been my involvement in communal and collective groups. In 1972 I was one of the founder members of a work co-operative; a year later Margaret and I and our two children moved into a house where we lived with other people. Since then I have always lived more or less communally. The pros and cons of communal living and collective working are too large a subject to go into here, but for me, the opportunity to work out in depth how I can live and work closely with other people, and they with me, is a very important aspect of any group project. A commitment to communal living is a commitment to dealing with difficulties; if we didn't believe that problems between people could be resolved there would be little point in attempting to live communally. The assumptions behind communal living and the techniques we use to deal with our relationships have a great deal to do with love, trust, understanding, caring and compassion.

Another strand in my exploration is conservation and an

understanding of ecological principles. Ecology was a very new concept when I studied it as part of my undergraduate geography course in the late 1960s, but its importance struck me immediately. We started a student group at Durham called 'Comprehensive Approach to Earth's Resources' (David Bellamy was a leading light); we read books and wrote papers for each other's education. It would be going too far to say that we saw in ecology the concept of loving our environment, but understanding, caring and compassion were certainly in there somewhere, and I remember crying over passages from John Stewart Collis's *The Worm Forgives the Plough*.

Then in 1980 we moved to the Findhorn Community on the coast of north-east Scotland; it was at Findhorn that I started to come to terms with a spiritual approach to life. After a very religious year in my late teens (which may well have had something to do with lack of love) I hadn't given spirituality much thought. I found John Blofield's books on Taoism in my mid-twenties and was impressed by the simplicity and common sense of what I read. I also read Lao Tze and Alan Watts, and in spite of what I recognized by then as sexism and elitism, saw a great deal of sense in passages from the *Tao Te Ching* and *The Book of Changes*.

Findhorn didn't have much time for political analysis (it doesn't now; I think in general it's convinced that it doesn't need any), but paradoxically it helped me to make connections I hadn't previously noticed. Findhorn doesn't acknowledge many of my political realities — oppression, political power, economic inequality, discrimination, injustice, to name but a few — but it does acknowledge the importance and power of the individual, and that makes a great deal of difference in everyday life. It was at Findhorn that I was introduced to the concept of unconditional love. Simply put, the idea is that when we can love ourselves and other people exactly as we and they are, without restraints, demands, fears, expectations and assumptions, then our relationships become simple, uncomplicated, light, joyful and immensely rewarding. I learnt later that Findhorn had no monopoly on the concept; as far as I can tell it had crossed the Atlantic in the early 1970s with the disciples of Ram Dass and Bhagwan. In America it's big business — it is, for instance, a cornerstone of Ken Keyes' 'Living Love Way'. I'm sure many Christians would suggest that Jesus had had a large hand in formulating the concept of unconditional love, though the post-Jesus record is rarely very edifying where love without expectation is concerned.

There are instances where I didn't think very much of Findhorn's practical record on love either, especially where it touched on anything at all 'political'. When a Scottish peace march passed through Moray, the community issued a statement expressing support for individual people in their work for peace, but declining to take a stance on either side — 'We don't want to be involved in politics' was a phrase on many people's lips. At a community meeting, one member suggested that it was okay to buy South African oranges if we blessed them before sinking our teeth into apartheid profits. Yet my time at Findhorn taught me a great deal about people relating to each other, dealing with issues as they arose, working together in a close and sensitive way, caring for each other. Every week our work department would get together to meditate and 'attune', to find out how everybody was feeling, how we could help each other, what would make our time together easier and more enjoyable.

I learnt a lot of new words at Findhorn — some Californian jargon, some dubious pseudo-religious language which reminded me of my Sunday-school days, a variety of ways of hiding what people really wanted to say behind vague and apparently safe platitudes. 'I feel the energy between us isn't flowing' often meant 'I wish you would go away'; 'I'd like to share a point of awareness' was a condescending alternative to 'I want to tell you something you won't like'. But some of the concepts struck home despite my sceptical predisposition, and unconditional love was one of them.

It was also at Findhorn that I discovered co-counselling, a very fortunate introduction to self-help therapy. I recognized that not only was this a tool I could use with confidence both for myself and for other people, but I didn't have to compromise my politics to believe in its basic assumptions. Here was a technique that talked the same language as me and made complete sense. During my introduction to co-counselling I read Harvey Jackins' *The Human Situation*. Near the beginning it said, 'The natural emotional tone of a human being is a zestful enjoyment of life. The natural relationship between any two human beings is loving affection, communication and co-operation.'

This didn't accept the Findhorn compromise of saying, 'Can we love each other with pure understanding love?' and washing down a South African orange with a cup of multinational coffee without blinking an eyelid, nor was it Ken Keyes charging large sums of money to experience the Living Love Way (though Ken has since done a lot of important work in the anti-nuclear field). This was an introduction to a technique which works on vitally important issues, and which seeks to change patterns of oppression, prejudice and discrimination.

The contradiction of oppressive patterns and a will to improve human relationships is also central to the theory and practice of feminism. I can't tell exactly when an awareness of feminism entered my life; the process has been gradual. It goes back to a fairly non-sexist mixed comprehensive school where I expected that Marjorie Hamilton and Christine Lloyd would always beat me, and to my parents' expectation that I would know how to cook and look after myself. It was in 1979 that I began to read feminist literature avidly; this was also the year when I began to work on a book about relationships. The two are intimately connected.

Understanding, caring, trust — all are vital elements in the growth of consciousness brought about through feminism. I am enormously grateful to the courageous women, and the few men, who have insisted that a humane, egalitarian and aware way of relating is fundamental in creating a better world. Not that feminism has completely integrated love: as a subject of feminist debate love has remained largely untouched, but feminism has laid stress on understanding and changing relationships between people to acknowledge the equality and importance of the individual.

At Findhorn I started to lead workshops, another Californian invention. The first was a relationship workshop — we used co-counselling, drama, role-playing techniques, games. It was great fun and we did a lot of laughing, some crying and shouting, produced an amazing play, and ended up in the sauna. The people in it asked me if I'd organize another. In the second we dressed up, listened to each other (better than the first time), all felt good at the end.

I was asked to help lead a workshop in Norway. The workshop organizers knew I came from Findhorn, and suggested that my part of the activities should be to lead an exploration of unconditional love. It was a challenge, but I worked out a programme of counselling techniques, drama and meditation. I was working with two Americans (where are all the Norwegian workshop leaders? — probably leading workshops at Findhorn), a spiritual healer and a new games leader. Between us we had a very good week. For me the highlight was when the group divided into two — a men's group and a women's group. In the two groups we explored the ways in which we had been limited and hurt by our experiences of being women and men, and each group chose the things that they would really like the other group to hear. Then the two groups faced each other across the room and agreed to listen to each other. You can call it compassion, caring, trust, openness; certainly all those things were there. But if that wasn't love too, I don't know what is.

That was the first of the workshops upon which this book is based. Now is the place to explain how the book is designed, and to say something about the process of writing it.

My intention is to describe two processes which run parallel to each other. One is the story of a workshop. It's an imaginary story, and all the people in it (except me) are invented. But it is based on workshops that I have led, and there is little that I have described which isn't close to events that have occurred in one or another of the workshops. The other is my own mental process. When I lead a workshop I don't lecture much; the idea is for the people in the group to experience what's happening themselves — one thing about love that most people agree on is that you can't just talk about it, you have to experience it to know anything about it. At the same time, I don't want to perpetuate the myth that for some inexplicable or esoteric reason, love is not susceptible to reasoned analysis. So I need to examine why I do what I do in a workshop, why I think it works, and what benefits it has.

As you read *Making Love Work*, you'll see that the workshop passages are interspersed with a commentary — the 'theory' that goes with the 'practice' of the workshop. I've integrated the two so that the book doesn't read like two unconnected accounts; how far I've succeeded I'll leave to you to decide.

Writing this book has often tested my ability to think clearly and write honestly, and it has helped me to isolate some of the reasons why, especially at the beginning, I had grave doubts about doing justice to such an important subject.

The first doubt was that I was trying to explore something that just can't be explored. I desperately searched everything I could lay my hands on in which other people had written about love, to see if they agreed that love was tangible enough to be analysed. They said things like, 'Perhaps we like having an area of our lives that we cannot explain and are not expected to' (Jacqueline Sarsby) or, 'There is no one true love that is valid for everyone' (Russell Vannoy). Even Ken Keyes didn't come to grips with it — in the glossary of A *Conscious Person's Guide to Relationships* everything else is clearly defined, but 'love' only has a non-definition: 'Love is created when our perception (of others) is not being distorted'. As the frustration deepened I realized that everybody was saying how very important love is, but they weren't saying *what* it is. Love is, well, you know, love: you know what love is. I had to break through this doubt, so one morning I went for a long walk in the woods (it was mid-January 1984), and when I got home I lit the woodstove in my room, sat down at my typewriter, and did what I was worried couldn't be done. I set out to analyse love.

The second doubt was to do with the task of recounting in words the feelings, the sensations, and the enormous variety of exchanges and occurrences which happen all the time in a workshop — small and subtle yet extremely important. How could I possibly capture the nuances, the minute signs that somebody in the group needs attention, the almost intuitive connections that happen in a small group, often simultaneously? I've read other books which attempted to capture the richness and variety of a small workshop group, and I've often been disappointed. Could I do any better?

The third doubt arose in a big way when two of my best friends read the first draft of Chapter One. Gail read it and said, 'Yuck'; Margaret was slightly more supportive: 'I can see what you're trying to do,' she said, 'but it's awfully soppy.' I felt very embarrassed, but not surprised. Perhaps I could sell it to the Living Love Foundation.

Then I started thinking about love and soppiness, and the more I thought about it the more I realized what a political issue it is.

There's the whole question of feelings, and love is to do with very strong feelings. People, especially men, in a stereotyped patriarchal society deny having feelings, largely because feelings are considered to be weak and womanly. Anything to do with women is debased, so love (which is soppy) is attached derogatorily to women and systematically devalued. On the other hand, patriarchal capitalism makes a lot of money out of romantic love; men maintain their power over women through the institution of marriage, the linch-pin of romantic love, so it obviously pays to keep love in business, even though it is soppy.

The denial of the importance of feelings means that we've been taught as we grow up that any strong feelings are soppy. We have those strong feelings anyway (not believing in them doesn't make them go away), but we're embarrassed to show them, especially in public, and we're also embarrassed when we see other people having them. We pass our distress about feelings very efficiently to our children, and help them to grow up with the same problems. 'Kissing is soppy,' says my eleven-year-old daughter — she's learnt that the feeling of yuckiness is 'normally' associated with feelings of tenderness in our society. No wonder we're so confused about love.

The bad feelings we all have about soppines don't help at all when we are asked to distinguish between strong and positive descriptions of emotion on one hand and forced sentimentality on the other. I have no doubt at all that it is politically sound to criticize a Barbara Cartland novel for being falsely sentimental, but what do I do when I find it difficult to equate the integrity of the writer with the power of their words? When one of the founders of the Findhorn Community, Eileen Caddy (in a tape called *Loving Unconditionally*) says, 'The world needs unconditional love. All humanity needs this sort of love,' I cannot trust that integrity, even when the words on their own seem reasonable enough. Yet when the radical magazine *Ink* prints words which are not very different in meaning, but I trust the motives of the writer, then I can jump up and down and say, 'Yes, that's right!'

The words in *Ink* are:

Resistance . . . is also manifested in the desire for excitement instead of boredom, love instead of politeness. The desire for love, conscious of itself and what opposes it, would become a determination to transform the whole of human behaviour and its economic roots.

The feminist writer Lucy Goodison quotes this passage in an essay called 'Really being in love means wanting to live in a different world', and adds:

I would like to believe that it could. The first step may be to accept and know our own experience better, and to move outwards from there. We may be able to make the first step towards transforming our love from a bewildering passion for one person to a deep-rooted lust for all life. We can at least try.

Yes, yes, yes, Lucy, I think to myself, feeling excited and lustful (or am I just being soppy?).

Chapter One

An Experience of Love

I've arrived early, but there are several people here already. They don't know yet that I'm the workshop leader. New people, new place. The drawing room of a Victorian hotel this time, a big colourful rug in the middle of the floor, a circle of assorted but comfortable chairs. Somebody has lit the fire in the old-fashioned grate, which is just as well, since it's early October and none too warm outside.

Two women are talking to each other by the window. I can't see the face of the taller one, since she has her back to the window and the bright sunshine means that she's just a silhouette. She's doing most of the talking, explaining how it was difficult to get here this morning, wondering if it's going to be worth the effort. A good start. The woman she is talking to is small, quite plump, hasn't taken off her woven poncho. Ske keeps nodding, but says nothing.

By the fire stand two men, one dark, bearded, articulate, wearing a CND badge; the other in a suede jacket, neat, serious.

Oh good, here's Judith with the paper and pens. I'm glad my friend Judith decided to come, though I'm concerned about her reaction to all this love stuff. Concerned? That's feeble; I'm embarrassed that she might think I'm too spiritual, not politically right on, soppy (heaven forbid . . .). And here's Penny, the woman Judith lives with. 'I've sorted Tammy out,' says Penny. 'I think she likes it here. I do too, it feels good.' Tamsin is Penny's daughter, being looked after today by one of the people who run the centre.

And now a rush of people. A solid-looking woman in woollen

tights and kilt; a tall fair woman who walks into the middle of the room and looks round with pursed lips as if to check that everything is in order. A man with a thin face and a beard looks round the door, sees her, and they sit down together in the chairs nearest to the fire and talk seriously in a foreign language — German. An older man in a rainbow sweater, fresh-looking, with a big smile. I smile back. A younger man, thin, wispy beard and moustache, sits on his own opposite the Germans while everyone else stands.

They still don't know that I'm the workshop leader. How quickly people's perception of other people's roles changes. As soon as I say who I am they'll stop seeing me as one of them, they'll start having expectations of me. Count them, see if they're all here yet. Look at my watch. Five minutes late already. Here we go again, another love workshop. This one's called 'Unconditional Lovers: A Workshop about Learning to Love Each Other'.

'I'd like to start in a minute, please. Can we move all these chairs back to the edges of the room? Thanks.' I've started. They know who I am.

Hang on, there are only eleven people. Well, there's usually someone who drops out. 'Let's stand in a circle and hold hands for a minute.' As everybody is sorting out who they want to stand next to, the door opens again and a tallish woman with short hair and dungarees asks, 'Is this where the workshop is?' Everyone makes encouraging noises, so she joins the circle, notices that she hasn't closed the door, apologizes, closes it, comes back, rejoins the circle looking rather apprehensive.

'Take a few minutes to bring yourself completely to this experience, to this room, to this group of people. When you are ready, look at each of the other people in the group, make contact with them. Watch your breathing; be aware of your feelings.'

A room full of strangers; strangers to me anyway, except Judith, who I know quite well, and Penny, who I've met a couple of times before. Strangers, but I know that after two days together I shall know them all intimately, we shall have shared some of our deepest feelings, our worst fears, our expectations and our longings. As yet, though, I don't know them; as I look round I wonder what's going on behind those slightly worried smiles. I have a better idea than they do of what's going to happen during the next two days. What power.

The woman who came in late has her eyes closed. 'Can you all open your eyes and make contact with the other people here?' I say gently. She opens them, looks frightened, searches the group as if to look for a friendly face. They're all friendly. She chooses the woman with the poncho and smiles fixedly. The man with the rainbow sweater is very systematic; smiles at everybody in turn, doesn't give up until they've smiled back. The two Germans seem to be carefully not smiling at each other, though they are standing next to each other holding hands.

'Well, hello everybody.' How jolly I sound, I'll try being more sincere. 'I'm pleased you could all come. In a minute we'll introduce ourselves, but first of all let's do what we need to do to arrive completely, feel some of the feelings that are stopping us being totally present. Who needs to stretch?'

We all stretch. That feels good. A few of the more enthusiastic touch their toes. 'Who needs to shake?' We shake our arms and hands, our legs and feet. One or two people are obviously embarrassed. The man in the suede suit is giving a royal wave, the woman in the kilt doesn't move her legs at all. Penny, on the other hand, is really getting into it, and rainbow sweater is lying down on the floor to kick his feet adequately.

'Who needs to yawn?' We all yawn. It comes surprisingly easily; can't stop yawning. 'Who needs to shout?' No offers for a moment, then the German man puts his hand up. 'Okay, let's all help you shout.' We all shout, a variety of noises. A deep bellow from the German man, a real scream from the woman who was standing by the window. 'Let's all try opening our throats and mouths wide and doing that again.' The woman with the poncho takes it off; off too come the suede jacket and the late woman's cardigan. We all shout again, followed by a bout of coughing.

'Who needs to laugh?' Several offers this time. Most of us laugh. Judith doesn't think it's very funny, but rainbow sweater makes a face at her and she smiles. Wispy beard doesn't join in, looks very sad. 'It's fine if you don't want to join in,' I say. 'Just be with the feelings. Does anybody need to cry?' Apparently nobody needs to cry, though several people look sad very convincingly.

'Well done, everybody. Are we all warm enough?' A glance round the red glowing faces shows that the warming-up exercises have succeeded.

Time for introductions. We stand in the circle again, holding hands, and say our names.

Penny.

Glenys (woolly tights and kilt).

Paul (rainbow sweater; keen).

Ray (wispy beard, frightened).

John (me).

Margaret (ex-poncho; quiet but warm).

Maurice (ex-suede jacket; erect, self-assured. Social worker?).

David (CND badge, a good sign).

Sarah (who was late; looks more human now).

Anna (the screamer, critical — I realize that's not fair).

Judith.

Wolfgang.

Ursula.

We say our names again. Penny, Glenys, Paul, Ray, John, Margaret, Maurice, David, Sarah, Anna, Judith, Wolfgang, Ursula. Thirteen strangers no longer.

'Since this is a workshop about people loving each other, let's remember all the important people in our lives who aren't here, the people we love, the people who love us, and as we think of them and what they mean to us, let's go round and say their names.' 'Rosalind.' 'Kate.' 'Anne.' 'Peter.' 'Barbara.' 'Tamsin.' Round and round we go, remembering our friends and bringing something of them to our group. Somebody gets stuck, it's Ray. 'I can't think of any more friends. Oh yes I can, my mum.'

Next we play name games.

We sit on the floor in a circle, throwing a little purple cushion round from person to person. As we throw it we say our name; to begin with we throw it to somebody whose name we're not sure of, soon I ask if everybody knows all the names. Nobody says no, so we stand up and play 'Boom-diddy-boom'.

With the exception of one person, everybody stands in a circle. The object of the game is to remember who is next to you in the circle, and to be aware of when the situation changes. I stand in the middle of the circle, close my eyes, stick one arm out in front of me with a finger pointing. Then I turn round a few times, stop, and open my eyes. The finger is pointing at Paul. 'Left, boom-diddy-boom.' 'David,' says Paul without hesitating. David is to the left of Paul, and Paul managed to say his name before I'd delivered my final 'boom'. If you can't name the neighbour on the side asked for by the person pointing, or are too slow, it's your turn to go in the middle. I close my eyes and turn again; when I stop the finger points at Ursula. 'Right, boom-diddy-boom.' 'Um, Maurice,' says Ursula, just in time. A third time, and it's Ray: 'Sarah,' says Ray. 'No, Anna. Damn.' His turn in the middle.

Some of them remember names easily. Paul never fails, nor Judith, nor David. Sarah has problems, so does Wolfgang. Penny calls Glenys 'Glynys', and we stop for a few seconds until Penny has pronounced it to Glenys's satisfaction.

So here we all are, thirteen people, two days, one very complex subject.

What we do next in our workshop is extremely simple, but is so direct, and so contrary to the way we normally relate to other people, that many find it difficult to understand either why I do it, or why I think it works. We are going to find somebody that we have never related to before, have never seen until half an hour ago, and tell them how much we love them.

The rationale for this exercise calls for an explanation of some of my assumptions about the basic nature of human beings. I assume that the basic nature of human beings is to love each other.

If the basic nature of human beings is to love each other, why don't we do it? There is a multitude of detailed explanations, but the underlying reason is simple in essence, and can be expanded to cover the complex spectrum of human experience. What stops us loving each other all the time is that we set up blocks between us and other people which hinder that love. The blocks are often so immense that they seem much more real than the love which is being blocked. The blocks consist of fear, separation, mistrust, pain, rejection, non-communication, jealousy, oppression, misunderstanding, embarrassment. Yet I believe that despite all these obstacles, which put together appear to be the human condition, our nature is still and always to love each other, and that if we don't remember that, we deny the essence of being human. The blocks and obstacles between people need to be acknowledged and dealt with, but unless we believe in something beyond the blocks, why should we believe that the difficulties of relating are worth tackling at all?

There seem to me to be two ways of finding out about the experience of loving and being loved. We can look at the blocks, or we can imagine what things might be like if the blocks were not there.

The first way, looking at the blocks, is the way with which we are all familiar. A problem arises in relating, we look at it, deal with it as best we can, and move on to the next problem. This process, worked through with awareness, cannot be avoided if we are serious about learning to love.

One way in which I imagine the realization of our true nature, the process of learning to love, is to think of people having a core of clear creative intelligence, a 'heart of love' if you like. This core is surrounded by everything that blocks love, layer upon layer of mental and emotional and physical protection, painful memories, patterned behaviour. If we want to find that heart of love, we have to strip away the layers, dealing with all the pain and problems as each layer comes away, rip, like a stubborn sticking plaster.

Most of our weekend together will be concerned with peeling away these layers and dealing with the resulting feelings. But there is the second way, a way of experiencing love directly and immediately. That's what we're going to do now.

The twelve people sit in pairs on the floor. The sun slants through the tall windows, the fire blazes. The people in each pair face each other, hold hands, look at each other, relax. One person in each pair starts to speak, looking at the other tenderly and compassionately, giving them full attention. I sit watching Margaret and Ursula.

'I love you,' says Ursula to Margaret.

After a few moments she says it again. 'I love you.' A quick smile. An embarrassed twitch. 'I love you.'

Margaret looks away briefly, realizes what she has done and looks back at Ursula.

'I love you,' says Ursula again, quietly, questioningly. A tear forms in the corner of Margaret's eye. 'I love you,' reassuringly, sitting quite still but completely attentive.

Margaret starts to cry softly, but continues to look at Ursula.

'I love you,' says Ursula with an almost imperceptible nod. 'I love you. I love you.'

A smile appears through the tears. The slightest additional pressure passes from hand to hand. 'I love you,' says Ursula to Margaret.

Five minutes later they change roles. 'I love you,' said many times, carefully, meaningfully, sensitively.

The first signs of healthy scepticism emerged when I described beforehand what we were going to do in this exercise and asked if anybody had any questions. Maurice was the first. 'How can I say I love someone if I don't know them?' he asked, slightly aggressively. 'It just won't be true.'

I explained again carefully that this is a way of testing the hypothesis that our basic nature is to love each other. 'Try looking at it as an experiment that you haven't carried out before. I know we're experimenting with people, and that can be frightening, but as with any experiment it doesn't always help to stick with known solutions. Everybody thought you'd fall off the edge of the world until Magellan didn't. Most people think you can't love somebody you don't know, but maybe that's because they've never tried.'

'Well,' said Judith, 'I can see what you're getting at, but isn't it quite dangerous to ask people to do something like this which may well bring up a lot of emotion? Maybe towards the end of a weekend it's okay, but isn't it asking for trouble to saddle people with stuff they can't handle when we haven't yet built up trust and support in the group?'

'I've thought about this a great deal,' I replied. 'When I started doing this workshop I did leave this exercise until near the end, but as a group we never seemed to move as quickly as groups who do it at the beginning. I think it's because until you have some idea of the quality of relating you are aiming for, you can't imagine what being loved openly and unconditionally is like. You tend to get bogged down in the problems. As for danger, I feel it's unrealistic to expect to explore love and not find it scary. It is frightening to do things in completely new and untested ways. At the same time, if anybody wants very much *not* to do any of the exercises this weekend, I fully support them in that choice. Is that all clear?' Judith nodded.

At the end of the exercise, each pair spends a few minutes talking about what happened during their time together, what they felt, what it brought up for them. Then we come together again in a circle to share the most important experiences and feelings.

'Soft and vulnerable,' says Margaret, looking at her feet.

'Open, but a bit scared', says Ray. He's looking at his feet too.

'I feel as though I made a real connection with Glenys,' says Penny. 'I really surprised myself.'

'I feel close and warm and a bit shivery,' says Paul. He's still holding Anna's hand. Anna looks uncomfortable.

So what happened for these twelve people? Were they just acting, pretending they loved each other when they didn't? Were they being manipulated, forced to say 'I love you' to someone they wouldn't normally acknowledge at all?

That's maybe what was happening for some of them at the beginning. They were perhaps doing what they had been told to because it would have been embarrassing not to, doing it because everybody else was doing it. But as far as I can tell, by the end of the exercise most of them know, and know in a very immediate way, what it feels like to love and be loved. They have some idea that it involves being very open and honest, willing to be vulnerable and feel feelings, willing to make a connection with another person.

We stop for a break, but most of the group don't want to go away. They're too busy talking, holding hands, hugging, smiling.

Whatever this love is, it's very powerful.

Chapter Two

The Varieties of Love

Love is powerful, love is important, but love is notoriously difficult to pin down.

The most widespread and common context in which people use the concept of love is in intimate relating. More specifically, the conventional 'love story' involves two people, a man and a woman, who meet each other and discover something between them that's very deep and special. In a typically Californian definition, 'distinguished psychologist' Nathaniel Branden talks about 'a passionate spiritual-emotional-sexual attachment between a man and a woman that reflects a high regard for the value of each other's person'. This sort of love seems to be a chancy business. 'Love happens to you,' says Jacqueline Sarsby in *Romantic Love and Society*, 'it comes like a bolt from the blue, unbidden and unintended'. Cupid's dart, and Cupid is invisible. 'I couldn't help it, the first time I looked into your eyes I knew.' Romantic love holds enormous promise for millions of people — 'if only I could fall in love, if only I could find somebody' — yet the reality is often enormously disappointing.

Romantic love is big business, one telling reason why capitalist enterprise won't readily let go of it. Mills and Boon authors know what they mean by love, and so do the editors of *Woman's Weekly*, selling a million and a half copies every week. They mean ruggedly handsome emotionally-scarred men gripping beautiful women by their naked shoulders in a passionate frenzy of kissing. Their lips meet, her heart pounds. 'Darling, you know how much you mean to me. Will you be mine? Shall we . . .?' You know the rest.

Quite a lot of the rest is to do with sex. Nathaniel Branden and

Jacqueline Sarsby are quite specific about it; other commentators on love start off being general and philosophical, but by various routes realize that in the context of our society, if you talk about love you are going to have to deal with sex at some point. In *The Art of Loving*, Erich Fromm comes to it via orgiastic states; in *The Inner Eye of Love* William Johnston comes by a tortuous route involving heavenly brides and bridegrooms. The popular imagination has inextricably linked 'real love' with sexual closeness, and since sex closely rivals love for vagueness and confusion, the role of sex in loving is an extremely problematic area for most people.

The equation of love with sex, together with the speed and abandon with which both have been commercialized in the last two decades, means that 'love' turns up in the most distorted and oppressive contexts. 'Love centres' in Frankfurt, Amsterdam and Copenhagen are frightening, impersonalized places where men use women to fulfil their exploitative fantasies. When video pornographers produce *Lovebirds* and *Teenage Love*, 'love' has become the degradation of human closeness, a monotony of stereotyped sexual activity, and a travesty of the concept that love involves, in Nathaniel Branden's words, 'a high regard for the value of each other's person'.

The aftermath of the hot lips and the pounding heart could as easily be a marriage proposal, the conventional channel for 'real love' and the traditional happy ending. The dominant picture that most Westerners have of marriage is contained in the response of a London teenager to a questionnaire about love in Jacqueline Sarsby's book: 'People get married because they are in love and want to live together and to have children and make a home.' Centuries of tradition lie behind this view of the 'natural' state of the world, and it is only recently that many of the assumptions implicit in such a view have been questioned. Love equals marriage equals sex equals home. It's certainly very tempting. We all need love, we all need a home, most of us like sex when it's appropriate. In that case we obviously all need marriage.

Yet there seems to be something called love which is specifically not included in marriage. Here in *The News of the World* is a story under the headline 'Minister in Love Scandal' in which a politician and the politician's lover have been tracked to their 'love-nest'.

They're having a 'love affair'. But this is *free* love, you must understand, not the same as the married sort at all.

Marriage brings us conveniently to religion, since part of the process of getting married can be that you receive the spiritual stamp of approval. It's interesting to conjecture what St Paul would have thought of all these different conceptions of love. They are hardly what the mysogynist preacher had in mind when he wrote to the Corinthians about unlimited love which 'bears all things, believes all things, hopes all things and endures all things'. He was talking about the love of and for his god, but he must have been aware that he was using a word which already meant many things to many people. The early Christian mystics made the distinction between 'agape', or godly love, and 'eros', which C. S. Lewis tautologically defines as 'the kind of love that lovers are in'.

For Christians, agape means nothing without god as its object, but since in modern English we generally only use the one word 'love' to cover all its manifestations, it is common for Christian thinkers too to be confused about the expansion of love from agape into a wider context. In *The Four Loves*, C. S. Lewis attempted to clarify matters by producing four different and identifiable varieties of love, each with a convincing Greek tag: 'storge' is love of family, 'filia' is love of friends, 'eros' is love of lovers and 'agape' is love of god. It sounds reasonable, but the categories easily become blurred, god becomes confused with nature and beauty and what Freud called 'the oceanic feeling', and it gradually becomes apparent that while you can distinguish fairly readily between a relative, a friend, a lover, and (if your belief system contains such a concept) god, it's much harder to say just *how* the feelings of love differ from category to category.

The problem arises partly because it's not always clear whether a specifically Christian notion of god is being invoked. When taken in isolation, statements such as Thomas Merton's in *Love and Living* that 'love is a positive force, a transcendent spiritual power . . . the deepest creative power in human nature', or William Johnston's 'living flame, a love which has no reservations or restrictions', seem entirely laudable. Yet whatever claims may be made about their universal application, these things are written in the context of a Christian philosophy which when taken in its entirety does not automatically embrace other points of view. Christian philosophers,

especially those of a universalist or ecumenical persuasion, have
a tendency to pin the label of Christianity on to statements which
can readily be accepted by a wide spectrum of philosophies. But
taken in their Christian context, ideas like those of Thomas Merton
and William Johnston are of limited enlightenment outside that
religion, and it is important as an intelligent reader to be able to
say 'Yes, that much I agree with, but it does not mean that I have
therefore to accept the Christian's connection between love and
a specifically Christian god.'

Philosophers too have had a field day with love, but they are
rarely concerned with what it actually feels like to love and be loved.
They have separated it from other human emotions in an attempt
to discover its true and unique essence, just as the medieval
anatomists searched in vain for the seat of the human soul.
Philosophers, just as much as theologians, tend to analyse love
without acknowledging their partisan assumptions, and so it is
hardly surprising to find a philosopher setting love of god, love
of humanity, love of one's country or love of truth in a hierarchy
according to their personal interests. I find it fascinating that many
philosophers play down the intense emotions which accompany
'falling in love', and attempt to show that in terms of rational human
behaviour such an experience is merely infatuation, and has very
little to do with 'real' love. The Christian church has much to answer
for here too, often equating intense and short-lived feelings of love
with lust — 'the big lie which comes straight from hell' as a
contemporary pamphlet from the so-called Personal Spiritual
Renewal Series (a Roman Catholic publishing house) puts it.

The supposed impartiality of philosophical investigation also
hides the personal experiences of the philosophers doing the
investigating. Jean-Paul Sartre, in a particularly depressing passage
in *Being and Nothingness*, attempts to prove that 'I love you' can only
ever mean 'I want you to love me', and since nobody can ever
be sure that somebody else loves them, the search for love will
always be painful and ultimately fail.

Convention and centuries of tradition have created a very tight
knot of love, sex and marriage, carefully perpetuated and looked
after by the romance industry and the church. Even fairly radical
discussions of close relating, like Jessie Bernard's *The Future of
Marriage* and Jonathan Gathorne-Hardy's *Love, Sex, Marriage and Divorce*

still make it clear from their titles that however searching their analysis, their reference points are still part of that tight traditional knot. I felt a real twinge of distaste when I found that awful word 'newlyweds' in Susan Campbell's recent book *Earth Community: Living Experiments in Cultural Transformation*. Cultural transformation?

Yet a great deal of questioning has taken place in the years since the early 1960s. I grew up with the Beatles; they said a great deal about love. 'All you need is love,' they sang, 'Love is all you need.' I knew they weren't just talking about romance and getting married and settling down with a home and children. They went to India, experimented with drugs, meditated; crowds of people loved them. I watched *Woodstock* in a cold cinema in Durham and secretly wished I had been there. They knew about love — just look at them enjoying themselves, laughing, crying. Yes, there was a lot that wasn't so good too — the drug dependence, the rampant sexism — but it felt like a beginning.

I read William Schutz's book, *Joy*, and discovered the human potential movement; they seemed to know about love too, and didn't seem dependent on god and marriage to experience it. Now when I visit alternative bookshops (and even a few mainstream ones) I see rows of self-help books with titles like I *Deserve Love*, *Loving Relationships*, *Choosing to Love*, *The Freedom of Love*, and *Learning to Live, Learning to Love*. Books like this have helped thousands of people to understand and integrate their experiences of love.

The two decades since the early 1960s have seen a rapidly expanding awareness of the links between our personal lives and political structures. As the flame of feminism was rekindled at the beginning of that period, the women writers who fanned the fire were very aware that love could not be left out of any meaningful understanding of the personal as political. In *The Female Eunuch*, published in 1970, Germaine Greer devoted a whole section to love, showing clearly that while love is vitally important, the romantic tradition allots to women a role in 'love' which makes them feel helpless, passive and dependent. At the beginning of her chapter on 'Love' in *The Dialectic of Sex*, published in 1971, Shulamith Firestone wrote: 'A book on radical feminism that did not deal with love would be a political failure.'

Since then love has been conspicuous by its absence from political and feminist analysis, and only now is it edging its way back in, in that inexorable way that love seems to have. I feel excited by this recognition, because it links very important insights from self-help therapy, feminism, political activism and contemporary spirituality.

Two writers in a recent anthology called *Socialist Visions* are convinced that love has a place in political analysis: 'To love someone, to feel deeply committed and responsive, to sustain caring and passion, to be a friend without restraint, these are some of the unfettered feelings of love separated from ownership of another person.' In the same article quoted earlier, from a feminist anthology called *Sex and Love*, Lucy Goodison makes the link between the political and spiritual aspects of love clearly and succinctly:

> As an ineffable, intense and other-worldly experience, being in love has been compared to religious ecstasy . . . Alexander Lowen defines the soul as 'the sense or feeling in a person of being part of a larger or universal order', and sees it as the result of our body energy interacting with the energy around us in the world and in the universe, which gives the feeling of being something bigger than yourself. Perhaps the strong link which occurs when we fall in love can open us up to these wider connections. Perhaps it is an experience which opens the lines between ourselves and the world. In a culture which denies spirituality outside the confines of established religion, falling in love may have become unusually important as one of our few routes to an experience of the transcendent, . . . a distortion of a deep urge to love the world which through social pressures gets funnelled into one person. In this, falling in love typifies the contradictory nature of our experiences under capitalism and patriarchy, our efforts to be human in a world organized along inhuman lines.

'Would it be possible for Tammy to join us for a while?' asks Penny. 'She heard us all playing games and was feeling left out.'

'I don't see why not,' I say. 'Check with the rest of the group.' Nobody says no, but I'm sure that half of them haven't heard the question. 'Can you check again until you've got a definite response from everybody? It may seem pedantic, but you deserve a reply when you're being sensitive enough to find out whether it bothers anyone.' This time they all nod.

Time to play again, Tammy is delighted.

First we divide into two rows, kneeling and facing each other with enough room between the rows for someone to crawl through. This is a human-wash, similar to a car-wash. The person at the end of one of the rows starts to crawl along between the rows, and everyone else uses their hands to soap, scrub, wipe, rinse and polish them before they emerge at the other end, clean, well-washed, and rather dishevelled. Most of them are also hot and smiling, delighted at having had all that attention.

After her turn Margaret collapses on the floor laughing; the two people at the end of the rows, David and Ursula, spontaneously give her a final polish. Judith chooses not to do it: 'I don't want to be touched by anyone at the moment,' she says, and catches my eye. Penny, who's next to her, puts her hand lightly on Judith's shoulder. Judith smiles, obviously relieved that her choice not to participate can be so easily respected.

Now we form two small circles, six people in each circle standing almost shoulder to shoulder, with a seventh in the middle. The person in the middle stands with their feet together, firmly rooted to the ground, closes their eyes, and relaxes. Keeping themself as straight as a tree, they sway, let themself fall, are gently caught by sensitive hands and passed slowly to the other side of the circle. Trust falling. Being the one in the middle is a strange but pleasant experience as you are passed lovingly from hand to hand. Constantly falling, constantly being supported. Falling, in love.

Chapter Three

A Vision of Love

What we are going to do next is a meditation, a reflective meditation on love.

I used to have a hard time with meditation. For about a year a transcendental meditation teacher called Ruth shared a house with us, and many of my friends did the training. A gold-lined portrait of Maharishi adorned her wall, and for an hour every day a series of dull thuds would resound through the house as Ruth practised her 'siddhes'. It was too close to religion for me.

But nobody can be at Findhorn for long without coming to terms with meditation, and I appreciated the absence of pressure to 'do' meditation in any particular way. I discovered that it was enough to consider meditation as a way of spending quiet time with myself, letting my mind become still and reflective, relaxing into my calm centre. I still don't know whether I meditate 'properly', but 'properly' has ceased to matter.

Tamsin hands round the paper and pens — large sheets of white paper. Tammy is eight, bright and outgoing. She has chosen to stay for the meditation. 'I know how to meditate,' she says. 'Look.'

'Make yourself comfortable,' I say to everyone, 'and make sure that your pen and paper are close at hand for when you need them. Be in a position where you can be relaxed, but where there's no danger of going to sleep.

'In the middle of your sheet of paper draw a circle, like this, and write the word ''love'' in the circle.

'I'm going to lead this meditation, but I'm not going to talk all the time. There will be periods when I shall leave you to let your thoughts and feelings and connections wander wherever they want to go. The theme of the meditation is love; we shall be reflecting on love, letting the idea sit in our minds, moving in and out of the meditation and noting on our paper all the connections that our conscious and unconscious minds make with love.

'Try not to censor yourself. You'll probably make connections like joy and happiness and freedom, but connections between love and possession, feeling trapped, clinging, loneliness or sadness may come up too. Don't deny those connections. Nobody is expecting you only to write nice things about love; you don't need to please anybody.

'You can write down feelings, memories, people, thoughts, whatever is important to you. Every time you write something connect it with a line, either to the word "love" in the middle or to something else you have written, so that you can remember the connections you made during the meditation. Make a note of anything that's important to you — symbols, colours, pictures. Above all, don't worry about doing it right or wrong: there is no right or wrong, only different. Is everybody clear about what we're doing?'

Off we go. We let ourselves feel our weight on the floor or chair, become aware of our breathing, breathing out tension and breathing in calmness and peace. We become aware of our thoughts and worries and concerns, watch them, wave goodbye to them. We become aware of our feelings, watch them pass. We become aware of our still centre.

We visualize a white light in the centre of our attention, a light that grows until it fills our awareness. We take as much time as it needs for that light to fill our mind's eye. And now we see the word 'love' appearing out of the white light, noticing how it appears, the size and colour of the letters.

'Now let that word "love" sit in your consciousness, and let the images and memories, the feelings and the connections, places and people, come into your awareness. As the words come, open your eyes, write them down, then close your eyes again until the next words come. Take as long as you need, there's no hurry.'

Five minutes pass, ten. No sound but the crackling fire and the rustle and scratch of people writing. Maurice is writing and writing, looking determined. Margaret hasn't written anything, but she's not asleep; I can see her eyelashes twitching. Wolfgang, on the other hand, is probably asleep. He wrote a few words at the beginning, but I don't think he's with us any more.

'Just a few more minutes now. If there's anything you want to write down but haven't dared, or you've been pushing it to one side, now is the time to include it.'

Sarah's turn to write furiously. 'How do you spell nature?' whispers Tamsin to Penny. 'Just do it how you think it should be,' whispers Penny into Tamsin's ear. Ursula has noticed Wolfgang too; nudges him gently. He's pretending he wasn't asleep, and smiles condescendingly at Ursula.

'If you don't have your eyes closed, close them when you are ready, and return to an awareness of the white light. Feel that light expanding inside you, filling you with warmth and love. Be with that feeling for a moment or two.'

In the silence that follows, a large log of wood on the fire splits slowly lengthwise and the flames roar up the chimney. Several people smile, Tamsin laughs.

'Holding that feeling of love and warmth, bring yourself, when you are ready, back to this room and this group of people.'

Slowly, people open their eyes and stretch.

'Now, can you find two or three other people to be with, and we'll share the things that came up for us?' In each of the four small groups, people take it in turn to talk about their meditation experience, and what they have written on their pieces of paper. I'm with David, Penny and Tamsin.

David starts. 'It was a good experience. I don't remember having thought about love like this before. It felt quite calm and easy.' He tells us about what he has written: 'I started off with loving people, openness, trust, equality, understanding. People I love: Gina, Peter, Anne, Maurice. Thinking about Gina took me to sex, fun, sharing, warmth. Then scariness, not knowing what to do, help! Then helplessness, need, closeness, security, rejection, sadness. Then round here I got on to trees, mountains, cliffs, sea, Flamborough, Yorkshire Moors. That got me on to cosmic things, here: sun, wind, exhilaration, joy. Here's Greece, Tibet, Himalayas. Children, babies, smiling, laughing. Then I thought about working: writing effortlessly, flow, creativity, clarity. Mmmm, that's it.'

Penny goes next. 'I didn't write very much,' she says, 'but I did get into the feelings of love. It was wonderful, and very sad'. She has written her meditation experiences as a spiral round a heart with a flowery 'love' in it. 'Calmness, peace, oneness; emptiness, nothing, sad, everything; people, openness, connection, understanding; goddess, earth, togetherness; deep, transcendent, embracing, holding, caring; affection, warmth; dancing, spirit, friends.'

'Why didn't you say me, mummy? Don't you love me? I've put you.'

'Of course I love you,' says Penny, hugging Tamsin tight. 'You come into friends.'

Tamsin has been hiding her paper upside down on the floor behind her. Now she produces it proudly and waits for us to react.

'Who's Bart?' asks David.

'It's not Bart, it's Dart. The pen slipped. He's my hamster.'

'Where did you come across god?' asks Penny.

'Oh,' says Tammy, slightly embarrassed. 'They tell us about him at school. They say god is love; I knew you wouldn't like it.'

'I think the whole thing's brilliant,' I say. 'You obviously know a lot about love. I really like "muothr nechr".'

Tamsin is delighted with the response, and lies on her stomach beside Penny, colouring in the little hearts with different coloured felt pens.

My turn, and my list is rather like David's. I have fear and loneliness, support and compassion, confidence and strength. I have islands, sea, rocks, friends, the important people in my life. And I have chocolate. Tamsin thinks that's funny.

After fifteen minutes I ask each small group to choose one person to co-ordinate the next part of the process, to distil from all the aspects of love that the people in the group have come up with no more than eight words which cover the most important of these aspects.

Tammy wants to be the co-ordinator for our group, and suggests that the first thing on our list should be friendship. Everybody agrees. Soon our list is complete: friendship, openness, warmth, nature, sadness, clarity, understanding.

We return to the big circle again. I explain that we are going to write all these connections with love on one big sheet of paper, which will give us a picture of what love means to this particular group of people. Glenys offers to do the writing. The co-ordinator from each group gives the first item from their list and Glenys writes it down, then the second, and so on. As the list extends, some groups have said things that are already on the list. Other things are very close to what is already written down, and Glenys efficiently puts them together. Now we have some idea of what love means to us. The list reads:

friendship/compassion/understanding
sex/closeness/safety
strength/self-confidence/freedom
passion/joy/excitement
openness/vulnerability
creativity/clarity
flow/connection
wholeness
pain/jealousy
nature/peace
sadness/depth
loss/loneliness
calmness

At the top of the sheet I ask Glenys to write 'LOVE'.

I set out to define love; now I'm going to do it. The definition is perhaps incomplete, but I'm going to put together all these elements to produce a working definition of love, a coherent picture of this powerful and important phenomenon. I'm not expecting to get it completely right, but at least it's a starting point, something which can then be refined, amended or discarded if it proves not to be useful.

As far as human beings are concerned, love is the intelligent, creative, connective flow that links us with ourselves and with other people, in the knowledge that our fundamental nature is to be joyful, strong, self-confident, passionate and full of life, and to co-operate with, and be understanding and compassionate towards, other people, since we are all unique and equally important parts of an interdependent world.

Love between people is one aspect of the flow which links every part of what exists with every other part, acknowledging the importance and uniqueness of each part, while knowing that everything is part of a web of interdependence.

There are times when we are intensely aware of this inter-dependence; at such times our experience of the flow of love is strong and vital. At other times the weight of pain and loneliness blocking our experience of love is so great as to appear to be the only possible version of reality. The gap between our experience of being blocked and our profound knowledge of love sometimes expresses itself in deep sadness and longing.

The blocks to love — pain, fear, jealousy, powerlessness, anger, loss, separation, loneliness — are all very real and are important to understand, but are distinguishable from love even though they come instantly to mind when we think about love. The blocks to love arise from a denial of the basic elements of love. The process is often complicated and difficult to follow, but, for example, pain can be directly related to denial of personal power, and fear can be a result of the abuse of openness and vulnerability. Anger and jealousy can often be related to a refusal to acknowledge joy and passion. Loss, separation and loneliness arise largely from a fragmented view of the world which denies the importance of connectedness and flow. It is easy to be experiencing the pain of inequality and powerlessness and be told, and believe, that pain is the necessary and inevitable result of loving and being loved. But the pain doesn't come from the love, it comes from the negation of power, creativity and wholeness, the denial of love.

I'm going to put all these aspects of love together in a diagram, to show more clearly how they are all connected, and again I want to stress that this is only one way of looking at these connections. Within the inner circle are what I call elements of love; together these constitute what in Chapter One I called 'the heart of love'. In the outer circle are the blocks to love, the layers which have to be carefully stripped away before we find the heart. I've drawn linking lines between many of the parts of the diagram to illustrate connections, although there are many other links, and the borderlines between the different elements are necessarily vague.

Two questions immediately spring to mind. One is, which is more real, love or the blocks to love? The answer has to be both. Both are part of the same reality, which is the reality of the world in which we live. Political and sociological analysts have tended to concentrate on the problems — the blocks — rather than the solutions to those problems, solutions which usually involve an acknowledgement of the importance of the qualities within the inner circle of the diagram. On the other hand, spiritual thinkers and the human potential movement have often concentrated on the positive qualities associated with love, and tended to play down the obvious importance of what is blocking the expression of those qualities. The reality of our existence includes the reality of love *and* the reality of the blocks to love.

The second question is: why call this construction love? It could just as easily be called life, energy, wholeness, flow, creativity or understanding. The choice of 'love' as the label for the universal flow of creative intelligence is to a certain extent arbitrary. *Making Energy Work* or *Making Life Work* might have been perfectly good titles for this book, though I find 'energy' off-putting when used outside the context of physics, and *Making Life Work* is even more pretentious than *Making Love Work*. But there are two connected reasons for using the word 'love'. The first is that 'love' is immediately accessible to everybody, everybody has a good idea

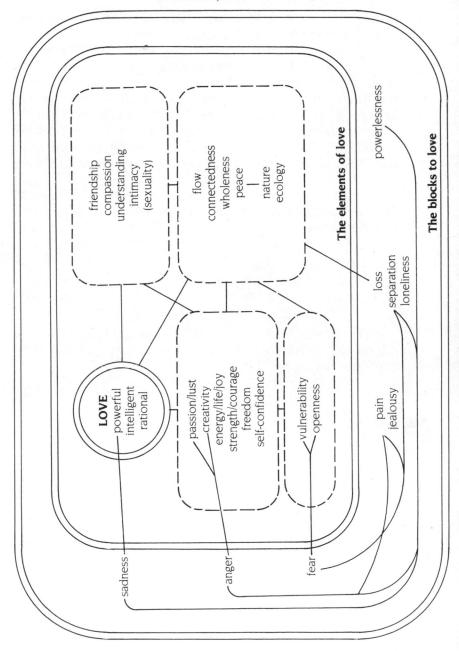

of what they mean by love and what love means to them. The second reason is that since it is a word in common use, and which, as we have seen from the meditation, people readily associate with so many different aspects of their emotional, mental and spiritual lives, 'love' has an immediate impact on people in a way that no synonym ever can. I can say to you: 'I feel the connection between us as part of the creative flow of the world' and it might explain very well what I am feeling, but it will never have the same impact on you as my saying, 'I love you.' Using the word 'love' achieves instant results; that's why I use instant miracle love in my meditations.

The next chapter is devoted to an examination in more detail of the elements of love. In the diagram I have linked these elements together in five groups:

> wholeness, connectedness and flow
> compassion and understanding
> openness and vulnerability
> passion, joy and creativity
> power, intelligence and reason

and this is the order in which I shall look at them. If you want to skip the analysis and come back to it later, the story of the workshop continues in Chapter Five.

Chapter Four

The Elements of Love

Love, wholeness, connectedness and flow

In our world, fragmentation is widespread. The legacy of our philosophical, scientific and educational tradition is that our view of ourselves and our environment is characterized by division, distinction and segregation.

The organic and non-organic worlds have been classified by scientists into genera, species and subspecies, compounds, elements, molecules, atoms and particles. Knowledge and skills have been divided into specialities and then into sub-specialities; no longer can you be just a scientist, a linguist, an artist or a musician, dextrous with your hands or good with people, not if you want to get on. You have to specialize, and there is no shortage of specialist education. From an early age, children can specialize in school subjects, which will help them specialize in their work, which will help them to succeed.

Division and distinction operate throughout human activity. Nations are distinct and separate entities with different governments, economies, currencies, legal and social systems. Politicians represent different parties with different policies. People belong to different classes, different religions, different races, and speak different languages. Old people are different from young people and women different from men; the rich are different from the poor and the owners different from the workers.

People are compartmentalized, labelled, and then limited according to their parentage, gender, age, work and loyalties. In a world where distinction and separation are fostered, behaviour appropriate to such beliefs becomes accepted as normal. Though the process of learning the behaviour is not always immediately apparent, we learn how to protect ourselves, our interests and our beliefs. We learn how to promote our interests and beliefs as being for the universal good, ignoring the possibility of alternative interests and beliefs. We learn to be secretive, devious, manipulative and non-communicative, and we come to believe that these ways of behaving are acceptable and inevitable.

In the extreme we are led to believe that people in different circumstances to our own are our enemies, to be shunned, discriminated against, feared, fought, and if necessary killed, in order to protect our interests.

A fragmented way of looking at the world often appears to be the whole reality of the situation. But this way of describing reality, this way of explaining our experience, overlooks some very important truths, and many people from their different viewpoints are realizing that a description of reality which stresses separation and division does not accurately reflect the way the world is and how we experience it. The development of an alternative explanation, which stresses connection, integration and wholeness, is coming together from fields of interest as apparently diverse as physics, philosophy, ecology, health, therapy, feminism, social and political activism, and spirituality and mysticism.

To begin with, a fragmented view of the world overlooks the interdependence of every aspect of our physical environment. Every part of our environment — water, earth, air, plants, animals, micro-organisms, human beings — interacts with every other part to create a living and ever-changing pattern. This ecological viewpoint stresses the connections between the different elements of the system, showing that things which might at first seem unconnected are in fact part of one interconnected and seamless planetary system. The discharge of sulphur into the atmosphere in central Europe and dying trees in Scandinavia may appear to be unconnected, but we know that the poisonous chemical, carried through the atmosphere, can fall again as acid rain thousands of miles away. In his book *Gaia: A New Look at Life on Earth*, John Lovelock speaks of our planet as 'a complex entity involving the earth's biosphere, atmosphere, oceans and soil, the totality constituting a feedback or cybernetic system'.

The links between sulphur discharge, acid rain and dying forests are well documented, though still denied by some industrialists. The complex social, economic and political connections which not only allow such discharges, but seem powerless to stop them, are far more difficult to understand. The fragmented world view encourages each person or group of people involved in the process to see no further than their own tiny part of that process, their own gains and benefits, and lets them ignore or disown the wider consequences.

The fragmented world view has many consequences at the level of personal choice. It may be convenient to buy whatever food takes our fancy, and the product bought from a multinational company in a chain supermarket may taste similar to the product bought from a food co-operative who obtained it directly from the farmer, but the implications of the different connections in each case are very far-reaching. Can the need for food really be separated from the exploitation of Third-World workers, a stockmarket which fills the pockets of for the most part already rich shareholders, the unavailability of land for subsistence crops to feed hungry people, and the ecologically unsound practices of monoculture? Defence expenditure is an example of a national choice which cannot ignore widespread global implications: not only does the allocation of resources to armaments perpetuate a politically divided view of the world in which unknown people are seen as the enemy; those resources are then unavailable for improving the general quality of life, especially for poor and less privileged people.

Many people actively involved in social and political change are beginning to understand that ecological thinking, social justice and co-operation are central to a world view which starts from wholeness rather than fragmentation. The recent growth and success of 'green' parties, the green symbolizing the connection with the earth, show that an awareness of the wholeness of human and ecological systems is expanding rapidly. Stephanie Leland, the co-ordinator of Women for Life on Earth, puts it well when she writes, in *Reclaim the Earth*:

We must turn our energies towards creating a consciousness of wholeness, in which we are concerned with relationships rather than difference, and in which we may learn best to live together and to cultivate the earth out of love and a conscious understanding of the harmony of life.

Physicists and philosophers are also experiencing the problems that arise when reductionism — reducing the world to smaller and smaller constituents — reaches its limits. While Newtonian physics, atomic theory and the laws of thermodynamics can help to explain many aspects of physical behaviour, the theory of relativity introduced a much wider and far-reaching perception of the world. Today, theoretical physics has to a large extent already outgrown relativity, and some very exciting suggestions have recently been made about the interconnected nature of the physical universe. Science still depends very much upon differentiation and specialization, yet the philosopher and physicist David Bohm is certain that the overemphasis on difference and comparison only leads to confusion. 'What is the use of attempts at social, political, economic or any other action,' he writes in *Wholeness and the Implicate Order*, 'if the mind is caught up in a confused movement in which it is generally differentiating what is not different and identifying what is not identical? Such action will be at best ineffective and at worst really destructive.'

David Bohm presents a view of the world in which physical matter and consciousness are part of an ever-changing flow in which both matter and thought are important but never static. He sees existence as a dynamic web of relationships, an unbroken wholeness in which every part enfolds or implicates every other part, in the same way as the illumination of any part of a holographic plate produces the complete image.

The same realizations and insights are gradually permeating the world of medicine and healing, as it becomes increasingly apparent that an approach to healing which concentrates on drugs, surgery, and the knowledge of specialist experts is insufficient. David Hoffmann, discussing the holistic approach to healing in *The Holistic Herbal*, explains it well:

> To truly heal, we need to look at the interconnectedness and the dynamic play of all the parts in the whole — the physical, emotional and mental bodies and the enlivening presence of the soul. And then we need to further expand our view and see this wholeness as part of a greater whole: the person's group, humanity, the entire planet, as all these work together in a dynamic, integrated system.

Spiritual teachers have been presenting a vision of wholeness and connected flow for a very long time. The teachings of Taoism, for example, centre upon the concept of ever-changing interconnectedness. One of the images of the Taoist 'path' is that of the stream, ever changing yet always one from source to sea. Flow, oneness, communion, wholeness and peace are ideas which occur time and time again in contemporary spiritual thinking; all show the growing realization of the importance of a holistic approach.

We all have experiences of wholeness and connectedness, times when the barriers dissolve between us and not-us, between us and another person, between us and the landscape of which we are part. We often call that experience love, and with love comes the rush of realization that we are part of a larger whole, an immediate knowledge of the connections between us and our environment, a sense of flow rather than struggle. We make contact with love.

Love, compassion and understanding

The feelings of separation and isolation that we all experience from time to time are often accompanied by a belief that one person can never understand what it is like to be someone else. The same upbringing that taught us that happiness and fulfilment can be achieved from competition and personal gain has also taught that other people's predicaments and problems are nothing to do with us. The awareness that people with different backgrounds and histories have very different experiences from our own is often accompanied by an unwillingness to find out anything about those different experiences. The difficulty sometimes arises from lack of opportunity, but just as often stems from a fear of change, of being threatened by somebody else's point of view, or of having our values and assumptions questioned.

The root of this fear and suspicion is an unwillingness to accept that we all share the same world, to accept that embracing wholeness involves acknowledging everybody on the planet as important, with an important perspective upon reality.

An important distinction must be made between the inability of somebody else to have our experiences, and the apparent inability of that person to understand our experiences. It's very easy when we are feeling alone and unsupported to confuse the two, and tell the person who offers to give us attention that it's no use because they'll never understand us.

Nobody else can have our experiences, and trying to live through somebody else's experiences is usually frustrating and disempowering. On the other hand, sharing fully and deeply with another person our important experiences and the insights that come from them is an essential part of human interaction.

For good reasons, this sort of communication is a rare occurrence for many people. Full and deep communication depends upon taking time for the recounting of the details of the experience and the feelings that go with it, and on the attentive listening abilities of the person to whom the experience is being recounted. Because we feel that people are not interested in us or willing to listen to us (feelings that are frequently connected with memories of not being listened to when we were young), we don't feel that the opportunities are there to share our experiences, so we don't share them. Our training in competitive conversation plays down the importance of attentive and open-minded listening in favour of interruption and winning arguments, and thus communication is thwarted from both sides. It's little wonder that most people only have one or two friends with whom they can communicate on any meaningful level, and that it is these people for whom they feel love.

A long history of separation and non-communication has led to what is considered today to be the perfectly normal situation where most people experience little real and deep contact with others. There is nothing at all natural about this way of relating, however. Any two human beings are capable of sustaining very real and meaningful communication, co-operation and compassion, given a willingness to believe that this sort of relationship, rather than competition and isolation, is a more intelligent and humane way of conducting our affairs.

At the very least, one person can always choose to listen carefully, non-judgementally and attentively to another person, however far apart their backgrounds and beliefs. They can choose not to interrupt, not to contradict and not to put down what the other person is saying. There is in fact no other way of learning about different experiences from our own in depth and detail. When space and time are allowed for a two-way sharing of experiences in this way, what frequently happens is that the two people involved start to have good feelings about each other — respect, empathy, trust, compassion, understanding, love. It isn't surprising that many people undergoing therapy or intensive care fall in love with their analyst or nurse; if you have been convinced that love, attention and caring are very rare commodities, it is very easy to fall passionately in love with the first person who gives you this sort of attention.

It is difficult to believe that this level of compassion and understanding can exist between any two people, but the simple truth is that it can. What is needed is a willingness to learn how to listen and give clear attention, and the courage to trust that our experiences are valid, important, and worth listening to. This willingness and courage is particularly important where there is a history of non-communication between groups of people — women and men, rich and poor, old and young, black and white. In order to work against oppression and discrimination we obviously need to do more than just talk about experiences; we have to act too. But without communication, and the compassion and respect that follow, we shall never be able to understand fully why we are acting, and we shall keep finding that while we think we are speaking knowledgeably on someone else's behalf, they will justifiably point out that we haven't understood them and their experience, that we haven't listened to them.

Love, openness and vulnerability

Being willing to listen to another person openly and attentively, or being trusting enough to share experiences deeply and honestly, involves lowering our defences, voluntarily letting go of the protective layers which separate us from other people. This can be frightening, because we can all remember times when we let go of our protection in the conviction that the situation was safe, only to discover to our dismay that it wasn't as safe as it looked. We got hurt, people didn't listen, they didn't understand.

It's a vicious circle. We remember so many times when we opened ourselves up, and were hit, that we are scared to do it again. When somebody does open up, it often feels very threatening to the other people around. It reminds them of painful experiences too, of all the times when nobody was there to understand *their* problems.

It is often difficult to conceive of alternatives to the destructive ways that people behave towards each other. It is hard to believe that distrust and fear are not fundamental to our human nature. Yet if we start from the assumption that a deep level of compassion and understanding can be created between people, the circle must be broken somewhere. This means being very courageous, and continuing to believe that communication and co-operation between people is fundamental to our nature despite the apparent iron grip of competition and opposition.

There seem to be many paradoxes about this way of looking at human behaviour. It involves looking at human interaction in very different ways from those taught to most children in our culture. All these things will be explored in more detail later, but let us look briefly at some of the assumptions we need to examine radically.

We need to rethink the concept of winning, when winning involves 'beating' somebody else, who is then a 'loser'. We need to rethink our ideas about right and wrong; in situations where there are two or more equally valid perceptions (and whose perception is not valid?), we get nowhere by refusing to let go of the idea that we must be right and therefore that the other person must be wrong.

We need to rethink the idea that personal strength comes from rigidity and 'sticking to our principles'. Every situation in our lives is new and different, and requires a new, different, flexible response. We need to rethink the widespread notion that real strength and real power come from the ability to force people to do what we want them to.

Strength and power, winning and being right, are all important aspects of knowing ourselves and what we are worth, yet they sometimes seem a long way from the openness and vulnerability which accompany a deep experience of love. This is because all these words can be used in two ways, and there is an important distinction between the sense that implies force, rigidity, opposition and a denial of love, and the sense that relates to wisdom, self-knowledge, awareness and an understanding of love. To use our strength against another human being, to take power over them, to win and make everybody else into losers, to be right at the expense of others, are ways of looking at human nature which deny our fundamental intelligence and compassion.

The alternative interpretation of these qualities shows how close they can be to the experience of love. When we experience love, and are able to stand aside from feelings of not being worthy of the experience, we know that we *are* winning, we know that we *are* right. These feelings of rightness and success are real and intense, and unlike the rightness of proving another person wrong or the success of beating other people in competition, rarely involve hurting or putting down somebody else. We can feel powerful without having any interest in having power over another person.

The connection between strength and vulnerability is perhaps one of the hardest for us, with our cultural background, to make. On my wall I have a Japanese brush painting which was given to me by a friend; it is a picture of orchids, and has the inscription: 'Strong like the Japanese orchid that withstands the wind and rain beside the waterfall.' The orchid is but one symbol from Taoist philosophy which makes the point that real strength and power come from the ability to be flexible and vulnerable, open and true to our basic nature. Another Taoist symbol is a reed in a storm — while trees and buildings fall around it, the reed bends with the wind and is still standing when the storm abates.

While being aware that strength comes from vulnerability, it is important to recognize that vulnerability does not need to involve any giving away of power. We sometimes confuse openness and vulnerability with the powerlessness of somebody whose freedom has been surrendered or taken away. To understand the relationship between strength and vulnerability, between openness and love, it is vital to remember that being true to our nature never involves losing personal strength; quite the opposite. This is particularly important if an awareness of personal power is a relatively new experience, or if we have a history of giving away our power or having it taken away by others.

Because of our legacy of defining strength in terms of force and rigid principles, to be open and vulnerable in love can make us feel very weak and helpless, a rare experience for people who are used to being forceful, strong, and in control of their environment. It takes a great deal of courage to go through the feelings of letting go of control, when it seems as though we shall never find a strong and powerful person inside the pain and distress.

We are frightened that we might lose ourselves for ever.

But we can never really lose ourselves; we are all strong, powerful, important people. The knowledge of this fact comes from the willingness to be open and vulnerable, to communicate and relate honestly and flexibly, to believe that love and compassion are part of our innate human nature.

Love, passion, joy and creativity

A long time ago I bought an old book of engravings by Gustave Doré, illustrating Dante's *Inferno*, *Purgatory* and *Paradise*. Hell and purgatory are fascinating places, full of eagles, poisonous snakes, phantom armies and naked writhing bodies. Heaven, on the other hand, is excruciatingly boring, with angels involved in endless formation flying. If heaven is where you go if you're good and loving, I'll opt for murder and revenge any day. The pictures of hell are far more interesting and exciting, and Doré and his engravers obviously had much more fun designing them. Yet surely sin and punishment, pain and torment, are far removed from joy and creativity. Why does hell seem so exciting and heaven so boring?

The confusion arises for several reasons.

The first confusion is to do with a misunderstanding about the place of feelings in human experience. The tormented souls in hell have feeling and emotion written on their faces; the angels in Doré's heaven are completely expressionless, like a rush-hour crowd at a main-line terminus. In a society where openness and vulnerability are considered to be signs of weakness and inferiority, any acknowledgement of feelings tends to brand a person as a second-rate human being. This is of course a complete travesty of our human nature: we all have feelings, and it's the blocking of feelings which creates situations reminiscent of hell. Children, who are frequently and condescendingly thought of as second-rate people, are constant reminders of the link between the flow of love and the display of emotion, but sadly we encourage them to grow out of it. Poets and artists are allowed an occasional vision of beauty and delight, but if a commuter on a train (especially a male one), looking up from his newspaper, were suddenly to exclaim, 'Oh, what an amazing sunset', it would probably have as much effect on the other passengers as paradise has clearly had on Doré's angels.

A second confusion is that since important feelings can't be completely ignored, some of the strongest human feelings have been subverted and used in exploitative and oppressive ways. They have been given specific and limited meanings and linked with antisocial behaviour; if there is money to be made from their manipulation so much the better. Passion and lust are rarely used nowadays to describe a deep awareness of the joy of living; they are more often the excuses for pornography and rape. As the words are limited in meaning, so the feelings they describe are devalued and narrowed. The equation of lust and passion with specifically sexual feelings widens the unnecessary gap which already exists between sexuality and the rest of our lives and, because the words are so widely associated with oppressive behaviour, creates problems when we want to express the joyful aspects of our sexual experience.

A third reason for the confusion between punishment and pain on one hand and passion and joy on the other arises from a widespread belief that experience gains validity and importance from being difficult and painful. Love is important, goes the argument, therefore it must be painful. Again, this is a complete travesty of the true nature of love, but the *chagrin d'amour* myth runs deep in our culture. The subtitle of a book called *Crimes of Passion* reads: 'Love, Murder, Torment, Lust and Heartache'. The 'pain is good for you' and 'the path of love is difficult and treacherous' arguments arise from a series of cultural beliefs which, although worth exploring, are of little practical value — beliefs in original sin and the innate imperfection of human beings, the puritan work ethic, and the romantic tradition of possessive love. As a result of these beliefs we tend to think of moments of joy, ecstasy and passion as very rare, and therefore very precious. They are certainly precious, but if instead of seeing pain and fear as the reality from which joy is a fleeting respite, we assumed that joy and passion were the reality of human existence, a reality which we block by protecting ourselves unnecessarily, how different our perception could be.

Part of this confusion of realities centres around our concept of excitement. The distinction is rarely clear-cut, but there is an important qualitative difference between the fear-excitement of screen violence, car chases, shoot-outs and feeling scared, and the joy-excitement of wide open spaces and the night sky, being in love and feeling exhilarated. Fear-excitement is felt in the stomach, is connected with feeling small, insignificant and scared, tends to be addictive in a destructive way, justifies aggression, violence, powerlessness and exploitation, has been exploited to the extent of appearing to be normal and natural human behaviour. Joy-excitement is felt in the chest (the link between joy and the heart is no coincidence), relates to expansiveness, vastness, feeling harmonious and creative, can only be exploited by limiting it, and is a much more likely candidate for describing the fundamental nature of human existence.

With passion and joy, a sense of wholeness and flow, comes creativity. We all know the difference between a project that is fun to do, interesting and fulfilling, when creativity flows out of our mind and hands, and times when we want to create something but there is no inspiration and flow, when creativity appears to be blocked. When we look at what is happening in such 'blocked' situations, there is often a clear connection between the block to creativity and the 'blocks to love' listed in the last chapter. Feelings of sadness, anger or fear, powerlessness or self-criticism, may have to be dealt with, and we can almost invariably unblock our creativity by taking space to feel these feelings.

When we understand what blocks our passion and creativity, and learn how to unblock them, we can experience real freedom. When love and creativity flow, it is abundantly clear that life is being lived to the full, as it deserves. In the introduction to Alan Watts' book, *Tao, The Watercourse Way*, the t'ai chi teacher Al Huang describes an experience of wholehearted creativity:

We were sitting on the library floor, comparing notes, nodding, smiling. Suddenly Alan jumped to his feet and joyously danced a t'ai chi improvization, shouting 'Ah-ha, t'ai chi is the tao, wu-wei, tzu-jan, like water, like wind, sailing, surfing, dancing with your hands, your head, your spine, your hips, your knees, with your brush, your voice. Ha Ha ha Ha, La La Lala ah ah Ah.' Gracefully he glided into the desk seat, rolled a sheet of paper into the typewriter, and began dancing with his fingers, still singing away.

Love, power, intelligence and reason

For us, brought up with a concept of love inextricably entangled with romance, marriage, home, sex and children, security and dependence, any idea that love is associated with power, intelligence and reason seems strange and unlikely. Surely love is about giving up our power — 'I felt weak at the knees, couldn't think straight, couldn't do a thing.' Love is blind — 'He looked at me and I felt so stupid, I didn't know where to look.' Love is completely irrational and unpredictable; it strikes out of the blue.

Despite these common misconceptions of the nature of love, the truth is that loving without restraint, loving openly and vulnerably, is not weak, irrational and stupid. To accept and respect somebody for no more and no less than the person they are, being willing to listen to and understand them, loving them unrestrainedly, is the strongest and most intelligent connection there can be between two people.

Because of our fears, it is convenient to believe that such loving is impossible except in very rare circumstances, but the power of relating to another person in the acknowledgement of shared love and humanity can produce apparent miracles in seemingly impossible situations. It is also convenient to believe that we don't have time to love people, or don't have the energy, or don't have anything to give other people. This, too, is to get caught up in the romantic ideal of difficult and time-consuming love. It takes no longer to smile at somebody than to scowl or ignore them. It takes no more energy to validate a person than to criticize them, though it probably takes more courage.

Love is very powerful, and love is also extremely intelligent and entirely reasonable. In an essay called 'The Politics of Intelligence', Andrea Dworkin talks about an 'active moral intelligence' which equates closely with my concept of unconditional love, and she too makes the important distinction between moral intelligence and love as 'a rarified relationship with one other person'. She writes:

Moral intelligence can only be developed and refined by being used in the realm of real and direct experience . . . Moral intelligence demands a nearly endless exercise of the ability to make decisions: significant decisions; decisions inside history, not peripheral to it; decisions about the meaning of life, decisions that arise from an acute awareness of one's own mortality; decisions on which one can honestly and wilfully stake one's life.

This intelligence is far from sitting back and waiting for love to strike, and being fearful and apprehensive. It is about taking action, taking risks, finding new and accurate responses to challenging and changing situations. An intelligent response to human contact acknowledges and respects both the connections and differences between people. It recognizes that we are all inhabitants of the same planet, sharing the same legacy, the same resources and the same common potential; at the same time we are all different, and every time two human beings relate the circumstances are never identical. Loving relationships thus call for sensitivity, flexibility and freshness — in short, intelligence.

The link between love and reason is frequently very difficult to comprehend. Love has been harnessed to a variety of limiting and oppressive practices and institutions, and reason too has not fared well of recent years. Love has been equated with emotion, and on the opposite pole has been placed cold reason, linked with justice, rigidity and principled discipline. Many people have watched the antisocial behaviour which has resulted with growing alarm, seeing how this 'cold logic' has produced 'cold people'; they have turned against 'reason' and 'logic' with a will, proclaiming, quite correctly, that what our world needs is to feel its feelings, to express its emotional life.

This is to ignore the fact that what has been labelled 'logical' and 'reasonable' by those who maintain power over other people is nothing of the sort. Crime, killing, aggressive defence policies, economic competition and pollution are the antithesis of rational behaviour; these antisocial and exploitative behaviours are the result of thoughtless and uncontrolled emotion, justified in the name of 'reason'. If two politicians consider themselves to be 'in opposition', the rational thing to do is to sit down and listen to each other, understand their differences, and work together to resolve them. Yet in the name of 'reason', coupled with 'justice' and 'democracy', these two people will instead sit on opposite sides of a parliamentary chamber and shout each other down. The rational behaviour of the leaders of two very different countries would be to communicate warmly and openly, work on projects where skills and experience could be shared, learn to understand and empathize with each other. Instead they have nuclear missiles poised to destroy the entire planet, the ultimate in blind emotion. In the name of 'reason'.

Reason means using our intelligence, the intelligence with which we have all been so liberally endowed. The rational human being is flexible, creative and sensitive, and recognizes the difference between blocked love and free-flowing love. In her book In the Name of Love, Jill Tweedie is convinced that 'true love is, above all, an emanation of reason; a rational apprehension of another human being'. She is right: love is the most reasonable way possible of comprehending the human condition.

Chapter Five

Breaking Through to Love

I have laid fourteen playing cards face down on the floor in the middle of the circle.

'Let's take some time before lunch to get to know each other better,' I say. 'We could introduce ourselves, but I'd like us to find out about each other in a way that requires more attention and more aware connection. We'll spend five minutes in pairs; for the first half of that time one person will tell important things about themself to the other, then we'll change roles for the second half. After that we'll return to the circle and tell everybody those important things about our new friend.

'Pick a card when you're ready; your partner will be the person with the same number.'

Paul and Wolfgang are first to the cards, Paul almost lunging forward. When everyone else has cards, Margaret is still sitting with her eyes closed; Anna passes her the last card and Margaret apologizes quietly. People hold up cards, sort themselves into pairs. I tell them when their five minutes starts, and the room becomes an indistinguishable babble of voices.

I'm with Maurice, who looks at me purposefully and starts: 'I'm Maurice Barrington. I went to school in Berkshire and then to Oxford University. Did PPE — politics, philosophy, economics. Moved to Leeds. I work as a community social worker. Live in a collective house with David and three other people. Very involved in politics; secretary of NALGO branch. I'm helping set up a skills-sharing co-operative — manual skills, for school leavers. Involved with Crèches Against Sexism. How long have I got left?'

'You've taken forty seconds,' I say, smiling.

Maurice nods.

'What else is important?' I ask.

'Ummm. Hmmm. Well, I like living in Leeds, though it's very different from my original background. My parents still live in Hampshire; my father's retired. I like my parents; my father doesn't understand a lot about me though. I visit them a lot more than they visit me. What else is important? I'm very busy. I actually work too hard. I get very involved in my work.'

'Time to change over now,' I say for everyone to hear. 'Thanks, Maurice.'

Two and a half minutes to tell Maurice important things about me. I tell him about the community I live in, my writing, the workshops I am doing, my children, my new bagpipes. It's surprising how much you can say about yourself in two and a half uninterrupted minutes.

'When you come back to the circle can you sit beside your partner, please? We'll take just one minute each to introduce our partner to the group. Who'd like to time people? Thank you, Anna. And who would like to go first?'

Glenys and Paul start to talk simultaneously. Glenys gives up first, but I ask her to continue. Positive discrimination.

'This is Ray. He's just left school and he's not working at the moment, but he's applied for a place on a job creation scheme as an apprentice carpenter. He lives with his mum in Hammersmith, but he'd like to leave home soon. He's very interested in working co-operatively and wants to set up his own co-op with some friends. Is that all right, Ray?' Ray nods enthusiastically. His turn.

'This is Glenys. Glenys teaches something, French? In a secondary school. She's worried about her job because they're doing something, reorganizing the school. She likes it the way it is. She's just come back from abroad with a load of schoolchildren, and she found it very tiring. Yes? Yes.'

'Thanks, Ray. Do you want to go next, Paul?' Paul shrugs, starts talking anyway.

'Sarah, everyone. Sarah's here because she wants to sort her life out. She's just had a baby, called Amy. She works part-time as a secretary; well, personal assistant really. She likes her work, but doesn't seem to have time to do it properly, and she's had hardly any time at all since Amy was born. She's very worried about her relationship with Jim, because he's having an affair with someone else — Jane? And the man she's working for, well, he's very considerate, but she doesn't know if she'll have time to keep the job on. Her parents are very worried about her, too, and she's thinking of going to see them next week, but she's quite frightened, because they don't know anything about Jim and Jane yet. Jim met Jane when they were on a conference in . . .'

'Time,' says Anna coldly.

'It's not all awful,' says Sarah quietly. 'I love being with Amy, and I'm sure my parents will understand. It's just . . .' She shakes her head, looks at the floor. Ursula, sitting next to her, puts an arm round Sarah, who starts to sob very quietly.

'That's fine, Sarah,' I say. 'Be with that sadness for a while and you can tell us about Paul when you're ready. Is there anything else you need now?' Sarah shakes her head, then 'A hanky' she adds as an afterthought.

'Who would like to go next?'

'I will,' says Judith. 'This is Anna. She's come with Margaret, who thought it would be good for her. She's a solicitor in London, Hampstead. She likes the work, though it's boring sometimes. She doesn't like the partner she works with very much; they've just finished a sort of relationship, and it isn't being very easy working with him at the moment. She lives in a small flat on her own, and she enjoys that. She sings in a choir, and likes opera. She's vegetarian, and she doesn't like children very much. She's enjoying being with a group of people for a change.'

Anna looks suspicious for a moment, then smiles. 'And this is Judith. Judith lives with Penny and Tamsin. She's a feminist and a lesbian. She's come because she's a friend of John's and wonders what a radical approach to love consists of. She says she's a sceptic. She works in a wholefood co-operative where she mostly does the accounts, and she's very involved with women's health things. She shares looking after Tamsin with Penny, and does a lot of cooking. That's my minute.'

'Can I go next?' asks Tamsin. 'This is Penny, my mum. I knew we'd get the same number. We both got sevens, and my birthday's on July the seventh. Seven seven, see? Penny looks after old people, she checks them to see that they're all right. She meditates every day. She likes *Mars* bars, but she pretends she doesn't. She has muesli for breakfast — yuck. I like *Rice Krispies*, but I don't put sugar on them. That's all.'

'Well done, Tam,' says Penny. 'This is Tamsin. She lives with me and Judith. She goes to Fullerton Road Primary School. Her teacher is Mrs Wood and her best friends are Ruth and Sanjeeta. The boys are all horrid except for Robin and David. She likes doing art and reading, and they've just been doing a project on India, and they made cut-out people in crêpe paper saris. She likes bright colours. She has a hamster called Dart who moves very slowly. It's a joke. She's enjoying herself here.'

'And next?'

'This is Margaret,' says David. 'She lives near Newbury, where she grew up. She's not working in a full-time job at the moment, but she's working two days a week in a bookshop, and she looks after two children while their mother works part-time. She says there's not much to say about herself, but it's not true. She reads a lot. She's just finished a book called *The Neverending Story* by a German author, and she liked it very much. She's going to read a book about pendulums next, because she's very interested in psychic healing. She's also become interested in the women's peace movement, and goes to Greenham Common quite a lot. Sometimes she has women who visit Greenham to stay, which she finds very exciting.'

Margaret looks embarrassed, as if all her secrets had been given away. 'Um, David. Well, David lives in a collective house in Leeds with a woman called Gina, and her son, who's called, um, something like Adam. David does a lot of counselling, and he leads a men's group, and he writes quite a lot. I think he's writing a book, and I think it's about oppression. That's all I can remember. Sorry.'

'Thanks, Margaret,' I say. 'You don't need to be sorry. You've done your best and that's fine.' Margaret is just about to say sorry again, but catches herself just in time. Several people laugh, and Margaret laughs too.

Maurice goes next, and then me.

'I'd like to go next,' says Sarah. 'This is Paul. He lives in Cambridge and he's a research assistant in the psychology department at Cambridge University. He's very interested in new developments in psychology, and he organizes a sort of therapy centre in Cambridge — I think it's called the Cambridge Natural Healing Centre. He does rebirthing and massage and Reichian bodywork. He's also done gestalt and psychosynthesis. He's just done a workshop at the Rajneesh centre near Cambridge which was called Zencounter. That gave him a lot of insights. Is that right, Paul?' Paul nods, smiling happily.

'Who's left? Ursula and Wolfgang. Who's going first?'

Ursula looks meaningfully at Wolfgang. 'I don't mind,' says Wolfgang. 'You go first.'

Ursula hesitates, then starts. 'I can't easily distinguish what Wolfgang told me from what I know about him already. He lives in a house in north London with me and his two children, Klaus and Maria. He was born in Frankfurt. He is forty-one. He is an engineer. He belongs to a Lutheran church and does a lot of church work. He is very interested in photographing wildlife. He is very much away from home on business. He works very hard. He moved to England five years ago to co-ordinate the work of a German firm and its British subsidiary. He likes England. He is interested in the new theology. He is . . .'

'Time,' says Anna.

'Ursula,' says Wolfgang. 'Ursula says that she is enjoying being here very much, but she is worried about the children, because it is the first time we have left them alone for a weekend. She says that she works hard at home, and for three mornings a week she works in an Oxfam shop, because she thinks this is very important. She would like to get away from the house more often, like this weekend, but she says that she finds it difficult when we have to co-ordinate our plans. Ursula is also very interested in spiritual things, and she reads many spiritual books. Her current fad, is that the right word? is called A *Course in Miracles*. She reads it every day. I think that maybe I have said enough.'

Ursula, in her bright red and white German skirt, is clearly angry, but she keeps her mouth firmly shut and smiles weakly. I look at her and catch her eye; she looks away. If there were time before lunch I would create a space to deal with the feelings that are so obviously coming up, but there will be time later.

One game before lunch. We stand in a circle, put our hands out in front of us, and close our eyes. Slowly we all move inward until we begin to feel other hands. Still with our eyes shut, we find a hand to hold with each of our hands. I open my eyes to see that everyone has found two other hands and see Paul with his eyes open; I suspect he's checking out which hands he wants to hold.

He finds one of Ursula's and one of Judith's, is satisfied, closes his eyes again. Unconditional love?

When everybody has found two other hands we open our eyes. The group has become one giant knot, and our task is to disentangle it without breaking the chain. One end of the circle soon sorts itself out; the other end seems impossible. Ray, Anna, Glenys and Sarah are tied in a tight knot. 'Ow!' cries Glenys as Ray's head appears under her armpit.

Nearly there. To disentangle the knot completely the whole chain has to climb through Anna's arms. For a moment she looks very tense, then starts laughing loudly. 'Careful,' she says as Wolfgang ducks under her arms and stands on her toes. Done, except that Maurice and Ursula, hand in hand, are facing out of the circle. I point out that they can turn round if they cross their arms, so we are all facing each other.

'Well done,' I say. 'Here again at two.'

Before lunch I spend a few minutes in the garden on my own, enjoying the autumn trees, the sun and the wind. I go over each of the people in turn, making mental contact, remembering the events of the morning, the signs, the feelings. It's a good group.

When I go in again, lunch is nearly ready. Penny, Tammy and Judith are standing by the window in the dining room, and Tammy runs up to me. 'I'm going out this afternoon with the children who live here.'

'Lucky thing. How was this morning for you?'

'Brilliant,' says Tammy. 'Didn't you like my drawing?'

I nod enthusiastically.

Penny and Judith are talking about Wolfgang. 'What a pain,' says Judith. 'Why didn't you pick him up on it? Men always get away with putting women down like that, and then other men support them by not saying anything.'

'I'd be very surprised if it doesn't come up again,' I say as the bell rings for lunch.

Behind us in the lunch line are Ursula and Wolfgang, talking in German in hushed but urgent voices. I don't know whether it means anything to Penny and Judith, who have pricked up their ears too, but I can't help but listen to their conversation.

'You said you'd do it,' says Ursula. 'Why say it if you're not going to do it? I was depending on you. It wouldn't be so bad if you hadn't said you would do it in the first place.'

'I said I'd ring at the end of the afternoon,' says Wolfgang through clenched teeth, 'and I will. If you need to know how they're getting on now, *you* go and ring them.'

'Scheiss,' says Ursula, breathing deeply through her nose. 'All right, I *will* do it. But I was depending on you. I'll go and do it myself.'

'You're always depending on me,' whispers Wolfgang after Ursula as she pushes her way towards the door. 'I can't stand it,' he mutters to himself self-righteously, helping himself to a plate of salad and coating it liberally with mayonnaise. He turns to take some of the vegetable pie, and the plate slips out of his hand, falls to the floor, mayonnaise side down. Wolfgang shuts his eyes, clenches his fists. 'It's *your* fault,' he shouts. He opens his eyes, becomes aware of the other people watching him, holding their breath.

Wolfgang stands helpless, motionless, mouth tight shut.

'I'll get a cloth,' says Glenys.

'Try breathing, Wolfgang,' I say. 'It always helps. What are you going to do now?'

Wolfgang raises his hand to his forehead, glares silently. Several people start to serve themselves again; Glenys comes with a cloth and bends down to start clearing up the dropped food.

'What are you doing, for fuck's sake?' says Judith. 'He dropped it.' Judith holds Glenys's shoulder, takes the cloth from her hand and thrusts it towards Wolfgang. Wolfgang is stuck. Glenys stands up, looks first at Judith, then at Wolfgang. Wolfgang takes the floorcloth and kneels down, picks up a lettuce leaf between two fingers, winces, looks up. But nobody except me notices.

At two o'clock Wolfgang and Ursula are missing.

'I saw them outside by their car,' says Ray. The door opens and Ursula comes in; she has been crying but forces a grin as she joins the circle.

'Is Wolfgang coming?' asks Glenys.

'I don't know,' says Ursula. 'I think he's sulking.'

Judith looks at Penny meaningfully.

We go round the circle, one word from each person to describe how they are feeling. Excited, tired, open, expectant, enthusiastic, tight, good, okay, good, warm, excited.

'Good. The theme this afternoon is support, acceptance and appreciation. Loving somebody without restraint means loving them for exactly who they are, respecting their strength and uniqueness, acknowledging the blocks to their awareness of that strength, and supporting their emergence from these blocks. First we'll build a mountain, a people mountain. While we do it let's be as aware as we can of being unique, important and independent, and at the same time being a vital part of the project we are building together.'

We make a mountain. The roots of the mountain are Penny, Margaret and Paul. The steep cliffs are David, Judith, Anna and Glenys. Sarah and Maurice form a ridge; Ursula and Ray curl up as foothills. 'I can't breathe,' gasps Penny; the cliffs ease a little. I add myself as the north spur and complete our joint creation with a pointing finger as a summit cairn.

Rocks and mountains, Ursula and Wolfgang, independence and dependence.

I've just finished reading Colette Dowling's book, *The Cinderella Complex*, the subject of which is the conflict, especially for women, of wanting to be free and independent, yet yearning to be looked after. Each of us is strong, powerful, free and independent, yet we have all been trained to be the exact opposite — dependent. It starts when we are children: 'Don't do that dear, it's dangerous'; 'Don't touch that, you'll get dirty'; 'Don't go too near'; 'It's all right, mummy's here'; 'Daddy will do that for you'.

There's no question that we all need help and support, especially when we are low or ill. Where it begins to go wrong, however, is when one person looks after another more than is necessary, usually as a result of fear and overprotectiveness. It tends to affect men and women differently because, as children and as adults too, we have been protected from different things. Girls are protected from the nasty, dirty commercial world outside the home;

boys are protected from having to do 'unmanly' nurturing and domestic work.

Young children do need to be protected from dangerous experiences, but there is a world of difference between support and control. They may be relatively inexperienced and need to learn a great deal about their abilities, but at the same time children are highly intelligent and can, if they are expected to, be very responsible at an early age.

Responsible and intelligent children grow into responsible and intelligent adults, but unfortunately the overdependence learnt in childhood is often perpetuated by our limiting assumptions about gender roles and the nature of institutionalized relating. Women are expected to leave their daddy's house and find another man to pay the bills, deal with the outside world and, as Colette Dowling puts it, provide a buffer between a woman and the world.

Men, on the other hand, are supposed to be tough and independent. The truth is frequently quite the reverse. Men have often become so dependent upon women for daily servicing and emotional support that, cast adrift in a world where they had to fend entirely for themselves, most men would find it very hard. In a world where women expect to be protected from harsh reality by 'their' men, and where men expect continuous mothering, it's hardly surprising that dependence is so troublesome and independence difficult to imagine.

The problem arises from two areas of confusion about independence. One is that independence is often confused with separation and isolation; the other is that dependence is often confused with overdependence.

Independence involves recognizing the strength and uniqueness of each person. It means respecting the differences between people while understanding and acknowledging their fundamental equality. It does not mean isolation or separation, though it sometimes involves being alone enough to appreciate our own individual strengths and qualities.

Dependence, on the other hand, means recognizing the connections between people, and understanding how we can provide each other with the attention, the warmth and the support that we all need. It does not mean dependence to the extent of believing that our well-being and happiness rely on the actions of someone else. I prefer to call the recognition of our connectedness with other people 'interdependence', because this describes more accurately how we can fulfil our needs without becoming overdependent, either upon individual people or people in general.

Ultimately, the understanding of dependence comes from an understanding of independence, from the conviction that while we all have needs, we are all strong and excitingly different, and it is precisely because we have this strength that we can help to fulfil each other's needs. The connection between independence, self-confidence and love is made at the end of *The Cinderella Complex*:

> The woman who believes in herself does not have to fool herself with dreams of things that are beyond her capabilities. At the same time, she does not waver in the face of those tasks for which she's competent and prepared. She is realistic, well-grounded, and self-loving. She is free, at last, to love others — *because* she loves herself.

And it works for men, too.

We are disentangling ourselves from being a mountain when Wolfgang decides to come back. I go up to him and give him a hug. 'Thank you for coming back, Wolfgang. That's a brave thing to do.'

We sit in a circle again, and I explain what I want to do next. 'I'd like to give a demonstration of how to support somebody while they deal with painful feelings, the feelings that block their love, their reason and their creativity. After that I'll talk briefly about some practical aspects of giving attention and support. Then everybody can have an opportunity to give and receive attention.' Wolfgang is sitting next to me, still tight and withdrawn. 'Would you help me in this demonstration, Wolfgang?'

'I don't know,' says Wolfgang. 'What does it involve?'

'I'd like to give you twenty minutes of attention; time for you to talk about what's happening for you, feel your feelings, in a safe space where nobody will judge you or interrupt you.'

'No thank you.'

'Sure?'

Wolfgang is silent. He has his hand to his forehead again, rubbing his finger to and fro across a bald patch. His mouth and eyes are shut. I take both his hands in mine. 'Wolfgang, are you there?'

Wolfgang starts to shake.

'Do you want to deal with this, Wolfgang?'

He nods his head.

'Okay. Can you open your eyes and look at me?'

He opens his eyes, but no more than to make narrow slits through which to glare.

'Open your mouth, Wolfgang, and make a noise if you want to.'

Wolfgang opens his mouth and growls quietly.

'Again?'

Nothing.

'I'll growl with you, Wolfgang. Ready?'

We growl together, starting quietly and getting louder. Then Wolfgang shouts, a deep painful shout. He pulls his hands out of mine and hits the floor on both sides. I put a big cushion between us. 'Do you want to try hitting the cushion, Wolfgang?' Wolfgang shakes his head, shuts his eyes again.

'Wolfgang? Where are you?'

'Angry.'

'Where are you feeling angry, Wolfgang?'

Wolfgang points to his stomach.

'Wolfgang, can you tell me about the first time you ever remember feeling angry like this?'

There is a long silence. 'I remember when I was eleven or twelve. My sister broke my aeroplane and my mother slapped me. I was very angry then.'

'Tell me about it again.'

'I made a model aeroplane out of wood and paper; it was very complicated. I left it on a table to dry when I'd painted it, and my sister smashed it. She did it deliberately. I hit her. My mother came in and didn't understand what had happened. She slapped my face. It wasn't fair.'

'What's your sister called, Wolfgang?'

'Gundel.'

'Tell me about Gundel and the aeroplane again.'

'I came in, and there she was in her wheelchair, smashing my aeroplane.' Wolfgang tails off, sinks inside himself again.

'What's she doing, Wolfgang?'

Wolfgang jumps. 'She's smashing my plane!' he shouts. 'It's mine! Stop it! Stop it. Oh, please stop. She's always right. She's in a wheelchair, so you'll have to look after her. Do be careful, Wolfgang. We depend on you to look after her. Remember she's not normal like you.' Wolfgang speaks like his mother, cold, reasonable, a hint of pleading. 'You must look after her. Poor Gundel. Poor Gundel. I'm sick of them depending on me! She's smashing my aeroplane!' he shouts. I hit the cushion hard. Wolfgang hits it. 'Stop it! Leave it alone!'

'What's going on here?' I say, as close as I can to Wolfgang's impersonation of his mother. 'Leave Gundel alone!'

Wolfgang screams and puts his hands up to his face. 'Ne, ne. Geh' weg!'

'Leave Gundel alone!'

He buries his head in the cushion and shakes.

'Wolfgang!'

He looks up, scared at first, then hits the cushion again. 'It wasn't me!' he shouts. 'It's her fault. She did it deliberately.'

'Look at me, Wolfgang, and say "It's your fault!" '

'It's your fault.'

'Again.'

'It's your fault.'

'Again.'

'It's *your* fault. It's *your* fault.'

'Is there a thought that goes with that?.'

Wolfgang thinks for a moment. 'Yes. It's: Don't blame me.'

'Say that to me.'

'Don't blame me.'

'Louder; keep saying it. Look straight at me.'

'Don't blame me! Don't blame me! Don't blame me!' Wolfgang's voice rises. 'Don't blame me! Don't . . .'

'Leave Gundel alone!' I shout, close to his face.

Wolfgang screams for a third time, sits bolt upright, and starts pounding the cushion. He screams for a long time, a high-pitched scream that gradually descends to a whine. He starts sobbing. Hand to forehead again. I take both his hands and hold them. 'Ooooh,' he whines.

'Good. Do it again.'

'Oooooooooh.' The corners of his mouth drop, and he opens his eyes slightly, as if to check that I'm still there.

'Ooooooooh,' I say.

Wolfgang's face crumples.

'Do you want a hug, Wolfgang?'

He sobs again, deep sobs. I move over to him and hug him tight, tight and still. Wolfgang cries; he cries just as he needed to when he was twelve but was never allowed. I hold him for three or four minutes, looking at him all the time. 'Well done, Wolfgang. That was very brave.'

He looks up. I ask him to look round the group and tell me everybody's name, to bring him back to the present. 'Okay, Wolfgang? Are you completely with us again?' Wolfgang nods.

I look round the rest of the group. Margaret is crying; Penny has her hand on Margaret's knee. Paul's arm is round Ursula, who is sitting with her mouth open. 'Well done everybody else for being so supportive.'

Time for a short break to stretch, run round the room, shake, feel some of the feelings that came up during Wolfgang's session.

We are sitting in the circle again. David is holding Wolfgang's hand, and Margaret, on the other side, has her hand on Wolfgang's leg.

'That was a demonstration of how to love and support somebody as they deal with some of the blocks to loving,' I say. 'Next I'm going to talk about some practical things you can do to support a person, but are there any questions before I do that?'

'How did you know what questions to ask?' says Sarah.

'I asked questions which kept Wolfgang with his feelings, partly by repeating things, partly by adding important detail, like his sister's name. I'll talk more about questions and directions soon.'

'Why did you keep saying his name, over and over again?' asks Ray.

'Because people usually respond immediately when they know they are being addressed personally. It constantly reminds the person you are supporting that you are there for *them*, and them alone.'

'I thought it was amazing,' says Margaret. Ursula nods.

This technique is called counselling, and I spend fifteen minutes talking about it.

Counselling is when two people choose to spend time together, where one or both of them are given a sustained period of loving attention by the other. Where the two people take it in turn to be counselled for equal periods of time, a common way of arranging a session, the technique is called co-counselling.

It's important to be very clear when the counselling begins and for how long it's going to go on. This is partly because it's always useful to be clear, partly because the counselling situation gives a degree of trust and safety which does not often exist otherwise, and partly because most people who counsel agree that anything which happens during the counselling session is completely confidential, thus increasing the safety and making it all the more important to know when that safety exists.

The purpose of counselling, in terms of a radical approach to love, is to support and affirm an awareness of the power of love, and to give space to look at and deal with the blocks to love. Practically, this usually means spending most of the time dealing creatively with the blocks, allowing and encouraging the person being counselled to feel their feelings, and affirming their insights and experiences of personal power, connectedness and creativity.

The basis of the technique is to give complete attention to the person you are counselling, and support who they are without restraints or expectations.

On a big piece of paper I write the basic do's and don'ts of counselling as I talk about them. On the 'do' side I write:

> DO — give attention (constant but not rigid).
> — listen.
> — make physical contact (sensitively, not intrusively).

I ask Judith to come and sit close to me, facing me. I hold her hands lightly, look at her eyes. Judith looks at me too, smiles, looks open and clear. Then I give her some rigid attention, staring at her with a fixed grin. Everybody laughs, Judith included. I show what it's like to be physically intrusive, gripping Judith's shoulders, putting my face inches from hers, invading her space. She pushes me off and retreats inside herself, closing her eyes.

On the 'don't' side:

DON'T — interrupt.
          — judge or blame.
          — advise or comment.
          — console or sympathize.

'Don't interrupt the person you are counselling, especially when they are feeling their feelings. They know what they need to do to heal themself much better than you do. I'll show you in a minute that not interrupting doesn't mean not being present and involved, but if the person you are counselling is clearly dealing with their blocks and coming to an understanding of their power, let them get on with it.

'Don't judge or blame the person you are counselling. This is sometimes difficult to remember, because judgement comes up in subtle ways. If someone says, for example: "I did a job really badly yesterday, and the person I work with realized I'd done it all wrong," it would be easy to nod your head, almost unconsciously. You might just be indicating that you'd heard what the person was saying, yet it could easily be interpreted as added criticism. Save your nods for supporting affirmations and insights into personal power.

'Similarly, don't advise or comment. If the person you are counselling says, "I just don't know what to do. What can I do?", you don't need to advise them, because they are the only person who can give the perfect answer to their own predicament. So don't say: "Well, if I were you I would . . ."; say, "What can you do?", several times if necessary. Empower them. And you don't need to say things like, "Yes, I had a problem like that, and I didn't know what to do either." Your turn to be counselled will come; the person you are counselling has enough to deal with without taking on your blocks.

'Don't console or sympathize — active attention is enough. If someone is crying, for instance, it doesn't help them to be fussed over and patted. I put my arm round Maurice, who's sitting next to me. 'There, there, Maurice. It's all right. Don't worry. Everything's okay,' I say, patting him and stroking him furiously. I can feel him recoiling and closing up. Several people laugh — it reminds them of similar experiences.

Back to the 'do's':

DO — repeat things.
   — use simple questions.
   — use the person's name.
   — ask the person to open their eyes, to keep breathing,
     and similar ways of opening physical blocks.
   — appreciate strengths.
   — contradict negativity.

'These are techniques to add to the "do's" we've already covered. Repeating what the person has said can sometimes be useful when they seem to be stuck. If they say, "It's terrible," over and over again, you might try saying the same thing back to them in an even tone, until they are ready to feel the feelings that go with the words. It's sometimes effective to ask them to repeat the description of an experience which has been painful for them; each time they repeat it they are likely to remember more of the relevant detail until they find the area of the block.

'Use simple and direct questions, and don't use the questions to lead the person you are counselling into areas of your own choosing. Trust the person being counselled to know what they need to do. Questions you might use are: "What's the feeling?", "What's the thought?", "Can you say that louder?", "What does that remind you of?", "Who do you want to say that to?" and "What do you want to say to them?"

'We've already looked at using the person's name. Techniques you might use to keep somebody physically open include asking them to open their eyes or their mouth, asking them to breathe, holding their hands to counteract a defensive posture, or encouraging them to make a noise appropriate to their feeling.

'We'll be working with appreciation more later. Appreciation is saying positive, powerful and loving things about somebody *to* them, or having them say empowering things about themself. Appreciation can often help the person you are counselling to overcome blocks by encouraging them to feel the feelings that get in the way of them believing in their power.

'A similar technique is called contradiction, which also works well in situations where the person being counselled is stuck and wallowing.' I ask Anna to help me in a demonstration, and she sits in front of me as Judith did.

'Anna, can you say "I feel awful" to me a few times?' She says it, maybe eight or nine times.

'What's the feeling?'

'Ugh. I feel depressed. Ugh.'

'Try "I feel awful" again.'

'I feel awful. I feel awful. Everything's terrible. It's true. Everything *is* awful. I feel *awful.*'

'Now try saying "Life is wonderful!" in an exultant voice, like this: Life is *wonderful!*'

'I can't.'

'Try it out. See what it feels like.'

'Life is wonderful,' says Anna in a depressed voice, looking at the floor, her hands together in her lap.

'Life is *wonderful!*' I say dramatically, flinging my arms into the air.

'Life is wonderful!' says Anna. 'No it's not, it's awful.'

'Life is *wonderful!* Let's stand up and do it together. Ready? Life is *wonderful!*'

I hold Anna's arms out, smile at her. 'Ready then? You do it.'

'Life is wonderful!' shrieks Anna. 'Life is *wonderful!* Ohhhhh . . .' The groan turns into a sigh; she closes her eyes.

'Life is *wonderful!*' I say again. 'Look at me, Anna.'

No response.

'Anna? Breathe, Anna.'

As she starts to breathe she sighs.

'Look at me, Anna, and make that noise again. Ohhhhh.' I take her hands.

She opens her eyes and sighs, a long sigh. Tears form in her eyes and roll down her cheeks. She sits and looks at me for maybe a minute, breathing deeply, tears flowing. Then she smiles.

'Wow,' she says. 'That was good.'

Finally, an important 'don't':

> DON'T — impose your own problems and neediness (remember whose time it is).

'Giving attention is not something most of us have been trained to do, so to begin with it can sometimes be difficult to keep your own problems and feelings out of the time you are giving to somebody else. But you *can* do it, especially when you know that your turn will come. If you ever get to the point where you feel you can't continue to give your full attention, maybe because it's reminding you too much of your own blocks, do tell the person you are counselling, so that it's clear to them what is happening, and you can maybe decide to stop or change roles for a while. As you learn to give attention, you'll find it easier and easier to listen to the person you are counselling without getting involved yourself.

'There's a story about a man who committed a murder. Eaten with remorse and guilt, he went to the first church he could find and confessed to the priest. "I've just killed someone," he said. "Oh my God," said the priest, "you'd better give yourself up at once. I'll ring the police." In a panic, the murderer rushed out of the church, but it wasn't long before he couldn't stand the pain and guilt any more, so he went into another church and found a second priest. "I've got something terrible to confess," he said. "I've just killed someone."

' "Hmmm," said the priest. "How many times has this happened before?" '

★　　★　　★

Time for a game. We play 'Huggybear'. We start by walking slowly round the room, anywhere we want to go. 'Mingle, mingle,' I say. 'Anywhere you want. Then when I say "Huggybear", you get ready to find all the people with the same characteristics as you in the area I mention. You'll see what I mean. Mingle, mingle.'

Everybody mingles for a few seconds.

'Okay. Huggybear, colour of hair.'

All the people with black hair find each other — Paul, Judith, David. A fair-haired group — Margaret, Ray and Ursula. Wolfgang on his own with almost white hair. Some in the middle not knowing which group to join, so create their own group. 'Here we go again. Mingle, mingle. Huggybear, star signs.'

Several people on their own, but two Scorpios — Anna and Maurice, and four Pisces — Glenys, Margaret, Judith and me.

Huggybear continues with other people thinking of things — people with children, colour of underwear, people in exclusive relationships. It's a very enjoyable way of finding out about people, and fast too. Finally I say, 'Huggybear, find somebody you haven't related to very much yet.'

I see Paul heading for Ursula, but Ursula quickly chooses Sarah. David asks Wolfgang; Penny asks Glenys. Paul tries again with Anna, and she agrees. Margaret and Judith look at each other and smile. Maurice and Ray are on opposite sides of the room, waiting. It's fairly obvious that they'd rather not be together. Ray takes the initiative, Maurice agrees.

'Is everybody happy about who they're with?' I ask, looking round and pausing when I get to Ray and Maurice. Nobody says anything. 'Right. It's your turn to love and support somebody unconditionally. Choose who's going to go first, and take fifteen minutes each. I'll tell you when the fifteen minutes are up. I'll put the "do's" and "don'ts" up on the wall to remind you if you need reminding, and I'm here if you need any help. Make yourselves comfortable, and begin when you're ready.'

I pin up the sheet, put more wood on the fire, then sit by it, listening to the noises in the room. The session starts quietly, but as people realize that they won't be heard individually, the noise level rises. After ten minutes I can hear somebody crying — it's Anna — and then Sarah screams: 'I hate you! I hate you! I hate you!' A good group.

'Time to change over when you're ready.'

The second half takes a while to get under way, waiting for the hugs and tyings up of the first half. The noise level is appreciably higher — David talking animatedly; Maurice saying, 'I'm too busy! I'm too busy! Sorry.' Ursula is crying: now she's shouting.

'Time to stop.'

Five minutes later, and we join hands in a circle.

'Thank you for the healing that has happened here this afternoon,' I say, looking round the circle. 'Break time. Fifteen minutes.'

Before I go out in the garden I find Wolfgang, and we hug each other warmly.

Chapter Six

Feelings and Actions

The break is longer than fifteen minutes. After twenty minutes I go through to the kitchen to see what's happening.

'I'm sorry,' says Glenys. 'I've been trying to get them to come.'

Paul is talking in the corner with Sarah and Margaret as audience. I hear him say, 'But of course, Reich wasn't completely right.' My right eye twitches and I smile. What's the feeling, I ask myself.

Five more minutes and we're all back in a circle.

'Right, I've got an invisible zoom here, and I'm going to pass it round the circle. If somebody passes you a zoom, turn round and pass it on to the person on your other side as fast as you can, keep it going quickly round the circle. 'Zoom,' I say to Margaret on my right. 'Zoom,' says Margaret to Anna. 'Zoom.' 'Zoom.' 'Zoom.' 'Ummm . . . zoom.'

'Well done. Now, if you are passed a zoom, you don't have to pass it on. If you want to you can stop it by putting your foot on the brakes like this.' I screech in best motor-racing tradition. 'When this happens the zoom goes back in the direction it came from, like this. Zoom.'

'Zoom.' 'Zoom.' 'Zoom.' 'Aaarrgh!' says David, pushing the zoom back to Judith, where it has just come from. 'Zoom,' says Judith to Anna. 'Zoom.' 'Zoom.'

Very soon the zoom is speeding round the circle, punctuated by a variety of screeches and screams.

'Great. Now let's see if we can handle two zooms at the same time. Zoom,' I say to Margaret on the right; 'Zoom' to Ursula on the left. The two zooms set off in opposite directions, are stopped and redirected, hit Ray at the same time. He's momentarily

confused, but disentangles both zooms and keeps them going.
Another two minutes and the zooms are irretrievably lost in laughter
and confusion.

'Feelings,' I say. 'We all have them, and they're very important
to us. Sometimes, though, it's not clear what they are and what
we should do with them.

'First of all, feelings are physical feelings — we feel them in our
body. When we feel a feeling, it's a sign that we should do
something with our body, something which acknowledges the
feeling and uses the energy of the feeling in a creative way. There
are appropriate reactions to all physical feelings, and they are
usually fairly obvious. If you feel anger you can shout, stamp, or
hit something. If you feel sadness you can cry or shake. If you feel
joy you can breathe deeply, sigh, laugh or sing.

'Feelings are important, because they are the body's response
to the way we interact with the world. Listening to our body and
being aware of what it is telling us can help us to respond accurately
to things that we experience.

'Feelings are good and positive, and if we want to live our life
fully they need to be acknowledged. Feelings exist to be felt.'

'What about negative feelings like despair and jealousy?' asks
Anna. 'How can they be positive?'

'I prefer not to think of any feelings as negative,' I reply. 'I think
that feelings like despair and jealousy have been labelled negative
because they often seem to be too difficult, or even impossible,
to deal with. If we believe in the power of love, though, and we
are convinced that our basic nature is to be creative and full of
life, we have to believe that so-called "bad" feelings are blocks
which can be overcome. Another part of the answer is that it's
not the feelings themselves which are difficult and negative, it's
the refusal to feel those feelings, and the belief that it's better to
suppress "bad" feelings than feel them.

'That brings us to a widespread confusion between pain and hurt,
and the feeling of the feelings which heals the pain. A child falls
over and hurts itself — that's the hurt. It cries — that's the healing.
But many people think that the *crying* is the pain, mostly because

it brings up painful memories for them. But no, the crying is the healing, and all the emotional hurt, and a good deal of the physical hurt too, can be healed by finding space and time to feel the feelings fully.'

'But you can't cry when someone in a shop is rude to you,' says Maurice. 'It would be so embarrassing.'

'You could, and a child would have no problem doing it. But we don't have to feel feelings exactly when they come up. We can choose to take them to a safe space later and deal with them then. Feelings that aren't fully felt at the time they arise get locked into the memory until they are dealt with, which is why it's possible to remember experiences from a long time ago and feel feelings that weren't fully felt at the time.'

'They get locked into the body, too, don't they?' says Paul. 'That's what Reichian therapy is all about, unblocking pain and tension locked in muscles and joints.'

'Yes. I think there's a very close connection between mental memories and physical memories, and the storing of pain in both. I also see a very close link between the storing of pain and the blocks to love. If we are not feeling our feelings, then we are very likely to be blocking our experience of love. Then it's very difficult to act in a clear, creative, flexible and intelligent way. We shall tend to act out of pain and fear in a very rigid way, which overlooks the fact that every situation is new and different, and calls for a new and different response.

'A very important thing to remember about feelings is that only I can feel my feelings, and those feelings are mine alone. Be very wary of anybody telling you how you should or must feel; they will almost certainly be projecting their own feelings on to you — "I'm feeling this, so you must be feeling it too." It's not true; there are no universal rules about how people *should* feel in particular situations. "It must be quite frightening to lead a workshop," somebody said to me recently. I thought about it, checked my feelings, and had to reply: "No, it doesn't feel frightening at all."

'Owning our own feelings and recognizing that they are ours and ours alone can sometimes be difficult, because we all learn at an early age to believe that other people "make us" have feelings. This is especially true of "bad" feelings, where we learn to blame other people: "When you tell me off it makes me angry"; "You make me nervous when you keep looking at your watch." If I am choosing to be creative and flexible, there is no way in which your actions can *make* me feel anything, not unless you are physically forcing me. I may be feeling feelings which are triggered by your actions, but the link between your action and my feelings is not inevitable and preordained. A useful exercise is to change blame to observation: "You said something about me, and I felt angry"; "You keep looking at your watch, and I feel nervous." When I do this, it helps me to become aware that alternative reactions are possible: "You said something about me, and I said how I felt about it"; "You keep looking at your watch; you are probably concerned that we shall be late so I'll let you know that I recognize the need to get ready quickly."

'Part of owning our feelings is recognizing that very often the feeling that comes up in a certain situation has little to do with what is happening in the present, which is an important reason for letting go of the idea that we can blame current events for our "bad" feelings. If an official is rude to me and I feel angry, almost all of my anger will be to do with encounters with other officials in the past where I didn't act clearly and creatively. In the present situation I can choose to feel anger *and* act calmly, clearly, creatively and intelligently.'

'It's all very well owning your feelings,' says Judith, 'but you can't say that situations and the way people behave don't make you feel things. If someone shouts at me I get angry. Anyone would. And I'd be right too. If a man shouts sexist rubbish at me it's my duty to be angry, he deserves it. It's too easy to say that it's all in *my* head. That man's *being* sexist. It's not just to do with *my* feelings.'

'That's a very good point,' I say, 'and I'd like to take a few minutes to look at it if everyone agrees. Does anybody object? Okay, to begin with I'll be the sexist man, Judith, and I'll work hard to try and help you to feel angry. Then you can counsel with David, who can give you full attention while you feel your anger. Then you can come back to me and deal with the situation intelligently and flexibly. How does that sound?'

'As though I let myself in for it,' says Judith, smiling, 'but okay.'

I sit opposite Judith and leer at her. 'Hello, love. Where are you off to then? Going out with the girls? Oooo. I bet you don't wear a bra; I'd like to get my hands on your lovely body.' I continue while Judith laughs, protesting that she can't take it seriously, but the laughing soon changes to a tight expression, teeth together, short shallow breathing. After two or three minutes I stop. 'Feeling?' I ask.

Judith nods: 'Angry.'

I motion David to take my place. 'All right?'

'I think so,' says David. 'What do you want to say, Judith?'

Judith knows what to do. She opens her eyes, puts her face close to David's and looks him in the eyes. David doesn't move, gives Judith full attention.

Judith takes a deep breath. 'You sexist shit,' she hisses. 'You creep. I'd like to take your puny little face and rub it into the ground.' As she talks her voice rises. She stops, breathes very deeply several times, then opens her eyes and shouts: 'Fuck you, fuck you, fuck you!', over and over, her fists drumming the words into the floor. Her anger bursts out into the room; I notice that several people are having difficulty breathing. After a minute or so Judith stops, breathless. 'Oh,' she says, 'that's better.'

I take David's place. 'Right, Judith. Deal with this situation. Here I am again. What are you doing tonight, then?' I look at her badge with the two women's symbols on a pink background. 'Oh my god, you're not one of those *lesbians* are you?'

Judith looks at me, her head on one side; shakes her head slowly and smiles a half-smile. 'You poor man,' she says, 'So much to learn. What do I want to say to you? Nothing. There is no way I'm going to take you seriously as long as you treat me as inferior. I'm quite happy getting what I want from women. Treat me as a human being or I shall have nothing to do with you.'

'Say that again, Judith.'

Judith continues to look at me, her head straight now. 'Treat me as a human being or I shall have nothing to do with you.'

I look at Judith, sit still for a few seconds, taking in what she has said, then nod to show that I have heard. I go back to my place in the circle.

'Feelings are there to be felt,' I say, 'but feelings are not always a good guide to appropriate action. Judith felt her anger, her totally justified anger, and was able to come back to the situation with an appropriate action. She could just as well have done it the other way round — dealt rationally with the situation and felt the anger later.

'I know the exercise we've just done may seem contrived, and it's quite likely that the action that Judith took wouldn't solve the problem of how to deal with an oppressive man, but I suspect that the action she did take was more rational and intelligent than being angry with a man whose likely response to a woman's anger is to laugh at it.

'By separating out the feelings from other people's actions, and owning them as our own, we can deal with the feelings that block rational and loving action in a safe and creative way. Then our intelligence and reason are free to act flexibly and inventively, which will almost certainly be more effective.'

Judith's example opens up a chain of thoughts for me about feelings, about how feelings have been denied and belittled for so long, about the way in which certain sorts of feelings have been denied for women and others for men, the whole area of sexual feelings and jealousy, and the issue of violence.

Because most people in our society are frightened by feelings, they pass the same unwillingness and fear of exploring emotion on to their children and to the people with whom they come in contact. Feelings are systematically denied, suppressed, laughed at and ignored. How often have we heard people (adults to children mostly) say things like, 'Don't cry' or 'It's rude to laugh', 'Quieten down' or 'Stop fidgeting'? Ignoring and suppressing feelings, however, doesn't make them go away. Unfelt feelings have very clever ways of demanding that their presence should be acknowledged. Headaches, depression, violence, boredom and irritability are just some of the ways in which unfelt feelings rise to the surface.

Everybody has feelings, and the range of feelings available to us doesn't vary much from person to person. We all know what anger, sadness, rejection, joy and excitement feel like. Yet although everybody experiences a wide range of feelings, convention decrees that only certain sorts of feelings are acceptable for certain sorts of people, and that they must only deal with them in acceptable ways. We have all been taught that some feelings are acceptable for women, and some are acceptable for men. Women are usually allowed to feel sad, helpless and powerless: they are frequently encouraged to feel those feelings because it supports the myth that women *are* weak and miserable. Women are certainly not allowed to feel anger, because anger is very unladylike.

Men are sometimes allowed to feel their feelings in the privacy of their own homes when nobody (except their overworked and frustrated wives) can see them, but the overwhelming belief is that real men don't have any feelings at all. Real men stand firm, don't flinch, steel themselves to the problems of living. They certainly don't cry, comfort each other, or admit to feeling weak and vulnerable.

These stereotyped expectations overlook the need we all have to acknowledge the full range of our feelings. Because the existence of the feelings is denied, the behaviour that results is frequently difficult to comprehend, and thought to be almost impossible to contradict. The 'blocked' behaviour becomes such an important part of the person's everyday experience that it appears to be nothing less than the way they are. A tell-tale remark in these circumstances is: 'I can't help it; I've always been like this.' The same beliefs lead to constructions of human behaviour along similar lines: 'Women are emotional', 'Men (often misleadingly extended to 'mankind') are aggressive', 'Pain is part of the human lot.' The 'people are just like that' justification of antisocial behaviour often results in a complete inability to act — a feeling (yes, another one) that the situation is hopeless, that we can't do anything about it.

Difficult though it may be to believe, the helplessness and hopelessness, being feelings, can be broken through by feeling them fully, and experiencing the pain and reliving the memories that go with the feelings. With a recognition of the blocks to love and power comes an understanding of the nature of that love and power.

In this light, conventional and limiting assumptions can be replaced with new insight. 'Women are emotional' ceases to be a snide put-down; it becomes an acknowledgement of the skills that women have in feeling their feelings, skills which help them to be powerful and wise. 'Men are aggressive' points to the obvious fact that most men have no other outlet for any of their strong feelings; if crying and screaming are disallowed, never mind joy and exhilaration, the only way that feelings can be expressed is by using the energy to destroy. While aggression and destruction have the consent of popular opinion — 'that's just the way men are' — violence will continue, but being culturally induced and politically condoned, violence can also be culturally refused and politically interrupted.

Pain is perhaps the most difficult of the 'I can't help it' beliefs with which to come to terms. We have become so used to thinking of pain as something that happens to us, completely unbidden and uncontrollable, that feelings of pain are often considered to be the only possible reality of a situation. The idea of original sin — it's our own fault that we are in pain so much of the time — doesn't help matters. Pain hurts; pain is real and important. But pain is not the only reality, and the idea that anybody deserves pain, whether through guilt or punishment, is a travesty of human intelligence.

We experience pain in our bodies; pain is a feeling. Sometimes there is a physical disorder which needs attention, but a great deal can be done about pain, even acute physical pain, by allowing ourselves to feel the feelings associated with the pain. The same analysis — feel your feelings fully, then act intelligently — applies to pain as to any other feelings.

Judith's demonstration also brings up an area of human behaviour which is frequently considered to be outside the realm of rationality — sexuality. It is a convenient belief, because it provides the justification for a great deal of behaviour which is thought to be entirely normal and natural, but which is in fact oppressive, insensitive, and inhuman. It reaches its extreme in sexual violence, but 'normality' excuses oppressive sexual behaviour at all levels of relating.

As with most 'problems' of human relating, we need to start by looking at feelings. Sexual feelings are part of the wide range of feelings which we all have from time to time. Close physical contact is often accompanied by sexual arousal for both men and women, though the less obvious external symptoms of arousal for women make it easier to disregard the feelings, which neatly complements the unfounded but conventional belief that women feel sexual feelings less than men.

The way we have learnt about sex has led to an enormous difference between what women think they need to do with their sexual feelings and what men think they need to do with theirs. Women have been taught to ignore their sexual feelings or sublimate them in romantic fantasy. Most men have learnt that if they are sexually aroused, the person who triggered the reaction is a prime candidate for shared sex: 'I can't help it; it was you that did it to me.'

Because sharing sexual feelings is so frightening and uncommon, we rarely feel safe enough to express them. We have learnt that sexual behaviour is so uncontrollable that if we have sexual feelings, we need to act them out by being sexual. Yet sexual feelings can be handled in exactly the same way as other feelings — 'feel the feelings and act intelligently' applies to sexual behaviour just as much as to other areas of our experience. Sexual arousal — a real and important feeling — never *has* to be acted upon. We are human beings, and human beings are intelligent. When we choose it to be, arousal can be only and simply arousal and nothing more, and something we can talk about and celebrate in its own right without having to extend the sexual performance to prove the existence of the feelings.

Because of the pain associated with our sexual experiences, we need to explore the blocks to loving intimacy in depth, and there will be a great many feelings of inadequacy, anxiety, powerlessness, grief and anger to be felt. But what follows is intelligent behaviour, behaviour which does not follow blindly the limiting assumptions that we have been taught about intimacy and shared sexuality. It acknowledges the other person as equally important yet excitingly different, as an intelligent human being with a mind and body of their own. It listens carefully to preferences and fears, and is not afraid of voicing its own feelings. Andrea Dworkin talks at length about sexual intelligence in the same essay that I quoted in Chapter Four; while I find her anger towards men brings up strong feelings for me, she speaks a great deal of wisdom:

> Sexual intelligence would have to be rooted first and foremost in the honest possession of one's own body . . . Sexual intelligence . . . begins with a whole body, not one that has already been cut into parts and fetishized; it begins with a self-respecting body, not one that is characterized . . . as dirty, wanton and slavish;

it acts in the world, . . . with freedom as well as with passion . . . Sexual intelligence is not animal, it is human.

Sexual arousal is a prime example of an area of confusion between feelings and actions. Another such area, and closely related, is jealousy. Jealousy is a feeling, but centuries of misunderstanding, often deliberate misunderstanding, have turned jealousy into an institution. As with the sexual lust that is popularly imagined to take a man over and make him unaccountable for his intimate behaviour, jealousy is frequently believed to be inborn in human beings, ineradicable from the human heart.

Jealousy is not inborn; it is learnt. It is rooted in a belief that one person can possess another, and has a right to limit the ways in which that person relates to others. This in turn stems from the fear of losing what nobody can ever possess in the first place — another person. Sometimes the feelings of fear and anger seem to be directly connected with the 'loss' of a person; behind this are often deeper feelings of losing contact with love itself. But not only does the abundance of love continue regardless; the love between you and your loved one is never in question either. They may be choosing to spend time with somebody else, and you may need to deal with the blocks to loving them that arise because of their choice, but the nature of love is such that there is no limit to the number of people who can share that love.

Common sense gives the lie to the idea that jealousy is an inevitable result of love. Two people who are unafraid of sharing their thoughts and feelings, who have an understanding of the connectedness and harmony of a loving relationship, are much less likely to stoop to violence and contempt when faced with dealing with each other's relationships outside their friendship. This doesn't, of course, mean that the feelings won't arise — recognizing jealousy as a feeling doesn't diminish the need to take it into account. But the feelings exist to be felt, and love between people cannot be limited. Emma Goldman, writing in 1911, knew the importance of this very well:

> All lovers do well to leave the doors of their love wide open. When love can come and go without fear of meeting a watch-dog, jealousy will rarely take root because it will soon learn that where there are no locks and keys there is no place for suspicion

and distrust, two elements upon which jealousy thrives and prospers.

'A space now for the feeling of feelings,' I say. 'It's often imagined that feelings always just happen to you, that you can't decide when to have them and when not to have them. It certainly needs practice, but it's not true that you can't choose. Somebody who is used to feeling their feelings will have little problem in crying or shouting, or dancing and leaping for joy either. And we can all learn to liberate ourselves like that.

'Let's go round the circle, say how we're feeling, and then express that feeling. If you need help, everyone else is here to help you.

'I'll start. I'm feeling tired after all that talking.' I stretch and yawn, a long yawn together with a sigh, then another yawn.

'I feel good,' says Maurice.

'How are you going to feel that feeling?'

Maurice pauses for a moment, thinking. Then he puts his arms out and his head back, opens his mouth wide and laughs.

Glenys says, 'I feel okay.'

'Okay. What's the feeling that goes with that?'

Glenys shrugs.

'Good. Can you do that again, but really dramatize it? A good stage shrug so they'll see you in the back stalls.'

Glenys shrugs again; the shrug turns into a stretch. She stretches her hands, then clenches them.

'Try shaking your hands quite violently.'

As Glenys shakes her hands she purses her mouth and breathes out deeply. She smiles.

Paul next. 'I feel tight in my stomach,' he says. 'I feel small and insignificant. I feel as though I want to curl up and disappear.'

'Try it.'

Paul lies down on the floor and curls up into a tight ball. After half a minute he uncurls. 'I can't stay like that for long. It's too embarrassing. Now I want to stretch.' He lies on his back on the floor and stretches his arms and legs.

'How would it be if we helped you, Paul?'

'Good.'

I indicate to the others that we're going to hold his arms and legs and stretch him, lifting him off the ground. Other people hold his head and body up. We pull, stretching his limbs. Paul groans with pleasure. 'Ooooooh. That's great.'

Judith's turn. 'I feel very strong and self-confident,' she says. 'I'm going to sing, very loud.' She sings the women's peace song: You can't kill the spirit; it's like a mountain. Old and strong, it goes on and on and on.

'Hmmm,' says Margaret. 'That makes me feel very excited and big. Can I sing it with you?' Margaret and Judith sing together, looking at each other. There are tears in Margaret's eyes.

Ray is next. 'It's all right,' he says, shaking his head. 'I don't know what I'm feeling. Just leave me out. I'm confused.'

'Where do you feel confused, Ray? Stomach? Throat?'

'In my head,' says Ray quietly.

'Would you let us help you to feel it?'

'Mmmmm,' says Ray, nodding.

I ask him to lie down in the middle of the circle, and everybody else to give him attention. Then I start to massage his head, finding where the confused feeling is.

'It's a sort of tightness right across my forehead,' says Ray. 'It's there a lot of the time.'

'Try opening your eyes and mouth very wide, Ray.'

Ray finds that difficult. I can feel his forehead sweating.

'Look at me, Ray, and make a noise.'

Ray lets out a strangled groan.

'Well done. Keep going. Keep making that noise.' I put my hands under his neck and lift his head slightly, stretching his throat. The groans turn to a shout, a tight-throated shout.

'Keep going, Ray. Try singing. We'll all do it with you.'

I sing a clear note and several others sing it with me. Ray sings. I stroke his throat, and the note comes more clearly. 'Well done, Ray. Keep going. You're a brilliant singer.' Ray is sweating all over. He keeps singing. After a minute or so he closes his eyes and relaxes.

'How's the feeling doing, Ray?'

'I think the headache's nearly gone.' He returns to the circle.

'I want to shout,' says Anna, 'see if I can feel some of my anger like Judith did.' She clenches her fists, tightens her face, and screams.

'Can I do that too?' asks Ursula. Her shout is more of a yelp.

'I'm feeling very restless,' says David. 'I think I need to move. Can I go for a quick run?'

'Good idea,' I say. 'Why don't we open that to anyone who wants to use up some energy? Three minutes run in the garden.'

It's started to rain, a light autumn rain falling from a darkening early evening sky. A run round the lawn is just what I needed too.

Back in the circle again, and it's Wolfgang. 'I feel very enthusiastic,' he says.

'How are you going to feel that feeling, Wolfgang?'

'I'm going to stand up and dance.' Wolfgang dances a short energetic dance in the middle of the circle, using his hands and arms in wide spreading movements. When he sits down, everybody claps. Wolfgang looks happy.

'That's a bit how I feel too,' says Penny. 'Joyful, energetic.'

'Show us what joy and energy feel like.'

Penny stands up, throws her arms up, starts to laugh. She laughs and laughs until tears flow down her face. 'Great,' she says joyfully, smiling and crying together as she sits down.

Sarah is last. 'Sarah?'

'I'm still thinking about negative feelings,' she says. 'I don't want them, but they won't go away.'

'Tell us about the feelings, Sarah,' I say, turning towards her.

'Jealousy. Fear. Frustration. Anger. Stomach feelings.'

I ask Penny to put a hand on Sarah's stomach.

'What are you frightened of, Sarah?'

'I'm frightened of dying.'

'What else are you frightened of?'

'Not being able to cope. Being alone. Being left. I'm just frightened.' She begins to shake.

'Lean back on Penny, Sarah, and carry on shaking. Exaggerate the movement.'

Sarah lifts her body several times, pushes with her legs and stomach, a stabbing movement.

'Open your mouth, Sarah, let the noise come. Keep shaking.'

She pushes again, her body convulsing, pushing up against Penny's hand. 'Oooh,' she sighs. 'Ohhhhhh! Ohhhh!'

I come up close beside her and hold her hand. 'Where are you, Sarah? What does this remind you of?

'Making love. Hospitals. Bed. Being alone. Ohhh!'
'What do you want to say?'
'Don't go away. Please don't go away.'
'They can't hear you, Sarah. Say it again, louder.'
'Don't go away! Please! Don't go away!'
'More.'
'Don't go away! Don't go away!'
I push down on Penny's hand.
'Owwww! Stay with me. Please don't go away!'
'We're here, Sarah.' I stroke her face softly. 'We're here. We're not going away. We love you.' I look round at the group. 'Let's all love Sarah.' We gather round her, link hands underneath her, and lift her gently off the floor. 'Let's all rock her and stroke her, give her attention and love her.'

The rest of the group hold Sarah, rocking her in their arms. Penny massages her stomach, I continue to stroke her face and hair. Somebody starts to hum softly, and others join in, harmonizing.

Sarah opens her eyes and smiles. 'Mmmmmmm,' she sighs. 'Mmmmmm.' She closes her eyes again. 'Mmmmmmmmmmm.'

Feeling her feelings, getting what she needs.

Chapter Seven

Appreciation

After a short break everybody is back in the room. It's beginning to get dark outside; we draw the curtains and bank up the fire.

A game before we start the last topic of the day. It's the steamroller game. Everybody takes off watches and jewellery and lies side by side on the floor on their stomachs, hands above their heads, like sardines. Glenys is on the end nearest the fire; I show her how to lift herself on to David, who is next to her, and then steamroll right down the line of backs until she falls gently off at the other end. There are a few groans as protruding bones meet sensitive muscles, but most of the noises are pleasurable. David next, then Penny, until everybody has steamrollered everybody else and the line of bodies has reached the cold end of the room.

When we have recovered from being rolled we sit, glowing both inside and out, in a semicircle round the fire.

'One of the best ways of dealing with the blocks to loving,' I say, 'is to validate and appreciate directly the love and power within ourselves and each other. Validation and appreciation mean saying and believing positive and empowering things about ourselves and others. This usually does two things simultaneously; it reminds us of those positive and powerful things, and at the same time it brings to the surface all the painful memories and feelings connected with the times and situations when our true loving nature has been invalidated, criticized, belittled or ignored.

'In an essay called "The Complete Appreciation of Oneself",

Harvey Jackins says that "the rational human being is admirable and approvable without limit". I'm sure he's right. He also says that any reservations we might have, any blocks to complete appreciation, are to do with rigid, repetitive, protective behaviours rooted in invalidation; he calls these distress patterns. Distress patterns attach themselves to a person and often appear to be inseparable from the person, but when you become aware of repetitive behaviour in someone which consistently "turns them off" and renders them incapable of flexible and intelligent behaviour, then you can be fairly sure that distress is in operation. And one of the best ways of dealing with distress is to counter it with validation and appreciation.

'Who's feeling in need of some validation?' I look round.

Ursula raises her hand. 'I'm still feeling bad about what happened at lunchtime. I'd like to tell myself that I really did do everything I could.'

'Right. Can we all sit so that we can see Ursula's face? We can all help her by giving her attention, looking at her approvingly, giving her the space and time to say exactly what she needs to say, and to feel the feelings that go with it. Okay, Ursula, tell us how well you handled the situation.'

'It wasn't easy. I was so angry I felt I couldn't do anything. I've been in that situation so often. I did what I could, but in the end I couldn't handle it. I don't know what to do in situations like that.'

'I handle my relationships brilliantly,' I say to Ursula proudly. She looks at me, puzzled. 'You say it: "I handle my relationships brilliantly."'

'But I don't,' says Ursula. 'That sort of thing always happens. I never know what to do.'

'I handle my relationships brilliantly,' I say to Ursula. 'Your turn.'

She frowns for a second, then smiles. Her face opens up. 'Oh, so that's a pattern. Rigid: I don't know how to . . . I get it. What do I say?'

'I handle . . .'

'Right: I handle my relationships brilliantly.' She says it in a small voice and shivers at the end.

'Sit up, Ursula. Put your hands out to your sides, maybe Ray and Glenys could hold your hands. Look up, smile at us. We know it's true. You do handle your relationships brilliantly.'

Ursula shivers again, purses her lips. 'I handle . . . I handle my relationships brilliantly. Ohhh.' She shakes all over, takes her hands away from her neighbours and shakes them too.

'Try saying it in a really pleased, smug way; total self-confidence.'

She takes the offered hands again, sits up, then shivers and hunches her shoulders, closes her eyes. 'Ohhhhhh.' A long shivery sigh.

'How do you handle your relationships?'

'Ohhhhh. Brilliantly,' says Ursula between clenched teeth.

'The whole thing now, Ursula. Ready? I handle . . .'

'I handle my relationships brilliantly,' says Ursula, her teeth still together and her eyes shut.

'Stand up, Ursula. Proud, exultant. It's true.'

'Oh my god,' says Ursula as she struggles to her feet. Ray laughs nervously. Wolfgang is staring at Ursula, unmoving. 'Right,' she says. 'I'm ready. What do I say? Oh yes. I handle my relationships brilliantly. Can I stop now?'

'Do it again, Ursula. When you've finished look at everybody, feel their support and approval.'

'I handle my relationships brilliantly.'

'Proudly, Ursula. Happy, pleased. Try it without nodding your head at the end, we know it's true even without you needing that extra bit of approval.'

Ursula nods, then smiles. 'I handle my relationships brilliantly.'

'Well done. Again, and keep your mouth open at the end as well as your eyes.'

'I handle my relationships brilliantly.' Eyes open, mouth open, she looks slowly round the group. She comes to Wolfgang, sitting stone-still with tears running down his face. Ursula closes her eyes and begins to cry; she holds the noise in behind tight lips. I move round behind her and put a hand on her stomach. 'Let the sound come, Ursula.'

She shakes her head. 'I can't, I can't. I can't.'

'Is that Ursula or the pattern?'

She puts a hand to her throat and opens her mouth. Immediately the noise comes, deep sobbing sighs. I take her hand and give it to Glenys to hold. 'Can you be here for Ursula?' I ask Glenys. 'Well done,' I say to Ursula as she sinks down beside Glenys and Glenys puts an arm round her.

★   ★   ★

Invalidation and the pain that comes from it extends far back into the mists of our childhoods. We have been blamed and criticized, told constantly about ways in which we were not good enough and the punishments that followed from not trying hard enough. The people who blamed and judged and criticized us learned how to do it by being invalidated themselves — the process seems infinitely self-perpetuating.

But now it's time to reverse the process of invalidation. Nobody learns well by being told all the time how badly they are doing. Nobody enjoys being beaten in a competition. Nobody benefits from being blamed; the past cannot be changed for any amount of blame. Nobody gains from being judged, for you can never step into another person's head to discover why they did the things which are now done and cannot be altered.

And it's time, too, to drop the useless belief that it is wrong to know ourselves to be admirable and approvable without limit. The idea that we should constantly deny and play down our strengths belongs to a deferential and hierarchical society whose demise is long overdue. We can be proud of ourselves without being proud at the expense of other people. Pride does not automatically involve setting ourselves apart and believing that we are better than other people. Pride — another word for it is self-appreciation — can simply mean being pleased with ourselves, acknowledging the things we do well. This won't necessarily feel easy, because we are working to overcome years of criticism and invalidation, but it is an infallible way of dealing with the blocks to loving ourselves.

This is another area in which the concept of reality can be extremely confusing, because patterned and blocked behaviour has for many people become the expected and 'normal' way of relating to themselves and to others. If somebody is truly self-loving, together with the pride and confidence that go with self-appreciation, many people are likely to find this behaviour quite threatening. They will explain that they don't experience the confidence as 'real'. 'That smile must be forced,' they will say. 'You can't be that happy. And I can't stand it when you ask me how I am every time we meet.' There are no prizes for distinguishing the creative, intelligent and confident behaviour from the rigid, patterned and blocked behaviour, though of course a rigid and inflexible grin is just as indicative of distress as a rigid and inflexible frown.

The heart of a belief in unrestrained love is that every human being is important, unique, intelligent, and capable of being very strong and powerful. A human being who is validated, appreciated and empowered can be extremely responsible, and can take full charge of themself and of the way that they respond to and interact with their environment. Every human being has this capacity, and it is part of our responsibility to help everybody to achieve self-empowerment. Part of this process is to question and contradict everything which suggests that a person is not in a position to be responsible for their own life.

The apparent 'reality' of blocked behaviour ties in with a prevalent belief in the inevitability of human failing. The widespread belief that we are all born with a 'flawed personality' would take too long to examine in detail, but I will look at a few elements of the belief, and at the alternatives provided by a fundamental belief in the power of love.

One idea that needs to be very carefully examined is that nobody is perfect, that we all have failings, things that we can't help. Phrases to watch out for are: 'I can't help it', 'I've always been like this', 'It's just the way I am.' This is the archetypal excuse for not changing, not moving, not dealing with things. It is a certain indication of a distress pattern, and can very often be an excuse for insensitive and antisocial behaviour. It's the excuse of the rapist and the murderer: 'I just don't know what came over me.' It's the excuse of the rigid mind: 'I can't change now.' It is no excuse at all.

Another belief to beware of is that criticism and judgement are an essential part of human interaction. Without criticism and judgement, the argument goes, nothing ever changes; for change to occur people and situations have to be confronted. This belief overlooks three important mechanisms:

— The past cannot be changed, only analysed. Change can only happen in the present and in the future.
— Confrontation leaves a distress pattern with no escape route other than defence and rigidity. Confrontation almost never

allows for change.
— Criticism and judgement often assume the 'right' of the judge
and the inevitable 'wrong' of the judged. In a situation like this
the distress pattern will fight to the death rather than change.

The alternative to criticism and confrontation is not to stand back
and let things happen, however. It is active experimentation with
creative reactions to people and events, using the techniques we
have already looked at — feeling feelings, owning feelings,
communicating intelligently and acting rationally.

Doing away with criticism and judgement does not mean being
less aware and perceptive, and perhaps I do the words 'criticism'
and 'judgement' some injustice by implying that they are always
used to support the critic's own 'rightness' against the 'flaws' of
the person being criticized, though this is more often the case than
not. I prefer to think of the appreciative and validating aspects
of criticism and judgement as discrimination and awareness, thus
acknowledging the importance of relating any judgement only to
our own perception, and not falsely universalizing it by implying
that our judgement is in any way a statement of a general truth.

A third related belief is that good and evil, right and wrong, exist
external to and beyond the influence of human beings. The concept
of an external fate is another twist of the 'I can't help it' excuse,
resting hand in hand with the limitations of religious predestination
and romantic helplessness. Every aspect of our being — mind, body
and spirit — is part of the connectedness which is the whole of
what exists; there is nothing external to it. Neither good nor evil,
right nor wrong, exist outside our definition of them. This becomes
very clear when we look at individual examples of personal
invalidation. A child comes in with a handful of beautiful daffodils
— the reaction of the adult who put a great deal of effort into
growing them is anger and frustration: 'You naughty, naughty child.
You must never pick flowers without asking.' Is the child bad or
not? Is its action right or wrong? Was its motive to please or to
defy? Where is the ultimate truth in any judgement of the action?

Finally, the 'I can't help it' argument is often used to maintain
inequality between people, and to justify the continued existence
of oppression and privilege: 'Women are just like that'; 'Blacks are
just like that.' This is an issue which will arise again in Chapter Nine.

For all the apparent reality of blocked behaviour, upheld by a belief in human weakness and failing, the real empowerment and acknowledgement of human beings comes from the process of appreciation and validation — loving myself and seeing the creativity and power in others. This doesn't mean ignoring the things I find difficult or have problems with, and it doesn't mean that things are so wonderful that they can't be constantly improved, but it does mean shifting the basis of my world view from a belief in inevitably flawed humanity to a belief in the complete appreciation of potentially strong, beautiful and powerful human beings.

It may seem excessive to demand complete appreciation, because it feels as though we should keep at least one eye on the 'truth' of the situation, which is that we all have things about us which could be better. There is always room for improvement, but there are several reasons why complete appreciation is philosophically and experientially sound, and why it works even better than partial, and seemingly more honest, appreciation:

— Who can possibly imagine the limits to human potential? As soon as we believe that we can appreciate only what we are, we limit what we might become. We can certainly appreciate things we have already achieved, but there is no logical limit to appreciation. Any fixed and rigid belief that we are limited is rooted firmly in distress patterns of limitation.

— We can never underestimate the pain and doubt caused by past invalidation. It is so clear that any reservations we have about ourselves are to do with past invalidation that we do not deserve to invalidate ourselves even further by believing, or feeling that we are being asked to believe, that our self-confidence and power can continue to be limited.

— Complete appreciation works. It is a dependable and well-tested way of reminding a person of those strengths and qualities which are part of their creative and intelligent nature, and at the same time of exploring and dealing with the things which block that loving nature.

As we choose to shift our assumptions about human nature from a belief in helplessness to a belief in power and validation, part of our new understanding will be that blocked love — patterned, rigid behaviour — is not the only available description of human behaviour. As the potential for free-flowing, loving, intelligent behaviour becomes apparent, we begin to see that distress patterns, while they 'attach' themselves to people and present themselves as though they *are* the person, are in fact patterns, and are not the intrinsically loving, flexible, creative person that everyone can be when they emerge from their patterns. The distinction between person and pattern, love and the blocks to love, is crucial; to treat anybody as though they *are* the pattern which has temporarily taken over is to continue to invalidate them as they have been so painfully invalidated in the past.

We go round the circle appreciating ourselves; a few seconds silence after each appreciation to let it sink in, to look round the circle and see that the whole group is listening to us, believing us, affirming us.

'I like my patience,' says Margaret.

'I like the way I am with Tammy,' says Penny.

'I like my hands,' says Maurice.

'I like the way I cope with things,' says Sarah. 'No. Yuck. I don't like that,' she says, grimacing. 'I like my strength. I *like* my strength.'

'Stand up and say it again, Sarah,' I say. 'Tell us again about your strength.'

Sarah stands up and plants her feet firmly on the ground, slightly apart. 'I like my strength,' she says determinedly. 'I am very strong.' Her whole body is tight; she has stopped breathing.

'Breathe, Sarah.'

She breathes a deep breath, blows it out loudly between her teeth.

'Well done, Sarah.'

'I like my sensitivity,' says Wolfgang quietly, choking slightly on the last word. He says it again.

'I like my ability to make good decisions,' says Anna.

Glenys next. 'I like . . . I like . . .'

'What's your first thought, Glenys?'

'I like my new purple tights,' says Glenys quickly, smiling.

'I like the way I am honest with myself,' says Ursula.

'I like my voice,' says Ray. 'Aaaaahhhhhh.'

'I like my beard,' says David, stroking it and lifting his head so that everybody can see clearly.

'I like my willingness and openness,' says Paul.

'And I like my tolerance,' says Judith.

Me last: 'I like the quality of attention I can give.' Deep breath. 'Two minutes to run round the room, go to the toilet, make up the fire, raise the energy before we appreciate each other.'

When we are sitting down again I say a few words about giving and receiving attention.

'The last exercise we'll do today is appreciating each other — saying positive, loving, empowering things that we have noticed about another person, partly because they are true, partly to counteract the invalidation we receive all the time.

'When you appreciate somebody, look at them, give them attention. Appreciate them because you want to, not because you think you ought. Be honest, true to your own loving nature. Be specific: "I liked the way you played with Molly and Tess yesterday afternoon" will usually provide more validation than "I like the way you play with children", even though both are true.

'Appreciate completely; there are many subtle ways of invalidating an appreciation. "This meal is wonderful" is more useful than "Your cooking *has* improved"; the latter can easily be taken as a judgement of the cook's past efforts. Avoid putting an appreciation down after you've given it: "I like that jacket very much; clashes with your trousers, though." Your listener will hear the criticism rather than the appreciation, so keep the appreciation clear and uncluttered. Remember that any reservation you have about complete appreciation is rooted in distress.

'When you are being appreciated, listen. You are being told the truth about yourself. We have learnt so many ways of brushing off appreciation that we need to be very aware of the ways in which we block the love that flows when we are being appreciated. Look at the person appreciating you. Open your body to that love — open eyes, open mouth, open hands. Be willing to receive. When the person appreciating you has stopped talking, take a few seconds, still looking at them, to take in what they have said. Then acknowledge the appreciation; the easiest way is to say "thank you". Try to keep still and relaxed while you're being appreciated, to give yourself a chance to hear what your body is saying to you.

'Enough talking; let's do it. When you want to appreciate somebody, say their name, and when you have their attention you can start, like this: Glenys, I love your brown eyes.'

'Thank you.'

A few seconds' silence, then David says: 'Wolfgang, I love your softness and vulnerability.'

Wolfgang looks wistfully at David and smiles a sad smile. 'Thank you.'

We spend ten minutes appreciating each other, our beauty, our power, our caring.

I look at my watch, the hand creeping up to six o'clock. Almost the end of our first day together.

'We'll stop for now, but I do want you to remember that you don't have to be in a workshop to appreciate each other. You have the rest of your lives to practise in.' Several people laugh.

'I'd like to teach you a simple song and dance before we go. The song goes like this:

> Heart to heart,
> Mind to mind,
> Body to body;
> It's a love divine.

'Can you remember that?' We all sing it several times, then I demonstrate the dance with Margaret. 'Heart to heart' is a short hug; for 'Mind to mind' we press our foreheads together. 'Body to body; It's a love divine' is a little dance, arms round each other's waists, before we pass on to the next person and start again. The song is a Sufi chant; it fits the theme of the weekend perfectly.

Everybody singing, moving round the room making connections with each other. Heart to heart, mind to mind, body to body. Loving without restraint, being true to our creative and intelligent nature.

The end of the day. People are hugging people as if they've known each other for years; talking animatedly in corners. Paul and Ursula are sitting by the fire holding hands, gazing into each other's eyes. A sudden thought: what if the whole world fell in love with itself?

Not much danger of that at present, though this little corner of the world seems to think it's a good idea.

Chapter Eight

Recovering the Past

A grey Sunday morning after an early night. I slept extremely well, and awoke from a complex dream in which I was attending some sort of conference, but couldn't get into the hall to hear the speakers. When I looked round the foyer, several people were sitting on the floor talking; Judith was there, and Paul, and several other people from the workshop and from my life. They were all naked, and when I looked down, I was too; nobody else had noticed. Hmmmm.

I have breakfast with Sarah, who tells me about the problems of finding somebody to look after Amy for the weekend, this being the first time she has been away from her for more than twenty-four hours. She tells me about the difficulties of fitting everything into her life, dealing with her job, which at least she can do at home some of the time, Jim's relationships, the baby, her parents. 'Being here feels like being let out, set free for a couple of days,' she says, looking up at me. 'It's really good; I feel more like myself again. If only I could do it more often.'

In the front room again, the fire is just beginning to catch and the lights are on to counteract the dull drizzly light from the window. Most people are here already, talking, wet hair steaming. Ray is jumping up and down in front of the fire shaking his arms. Paul looks at his watch. Penny is the last to arrive. 'Sorry,' she says, 'just seeing to Tammy.'

We hold hands in a circle and close our eyes for a minute or so. I can feel Ursula's cold hand to my left, Glenys's warm soft hand to my right. I listen to the breathing and the crackle of the fire.

'When you are ready, open your eyes and make contact with each of the other people in the room.' I take time to look at each person and smile; good to see you all again.

'Okay, it's game time again. Find a partner and sit down with them. Make sure you have some space round you.'

We're going to play 'People to People', a sure way to warm up a group at the beginning of a session, and an excellent game to bring people close to each other. 'When I say two parts of the body, what you have to do is bring those parts into contact with each other. So if I say "finger to nose", for example, you each put a finger on the other person's nose. It's very easy. Let's see how we get on.'

I start with a few easy ones — 'nose to nose', 'arm to back', 'cheek to cheek'. Then some which involve more contact with the ground: 'knee to neck', 'toe to chin'. One or two warm and intimate poses — 'ear to mouth', 'back of knee to bottom' — then 'When I say "people to people", everybody needs to find a new partner, and the person without a partner becomes the caller. So, people to people.'

Arms reach out to grab people in new pairs; Ray ends up on his own, looking lost. However, he's an inventive caller: 'lips to nose', 'foot to back of head', 'ear to stomach', 'people to people'.

Five minutes of closeness later we are ready to start the next exercise. We are going to meditate again, this time using a technique called guided fantasy or guided imagery. I ask everybody to find a comfortable position to meditate in, a position which they can stay in for twenty or twenty-five minutes. I ask them to have pen and paper handy if they need it, and to make sure they will be warm enough. Paul goes to fetch a pile of blankets; soon everybody is settled and the room is quiet.

'If you haven't already, close your eyes, and when you are ready take two or three deep breaths. Breathe your lungs full, then let the air out completely. Be very aware of your breathing.' Wolfgang coughs, then frowns.

'Gradually become aware of the ground or the chair under you, the way your body is sitting, what your body is doing. Listen to the sounds in the room. Be with these physical sensations for a while.'

Time passes. 'Your body is part of you, but you are not only your body.

'Now become aware of any feelings you are feeling right now. Don't judge them, just feel them, watch them forming and passing, be with them.'

Time passes. 'Your feelings are part of you, but you are not only your feelings.

'Now become aware of your thoughts; see them passing through your mind, one after another, like clouds. Don't stop to analyse them, just watch them come and go.'

Time passes. 'Your thoughts are part of you, but you are not only your thoughts.

'You are all these things, and more. You are your self, a centre of pure consciousness, observing your body, your feelings, your thoughts. Clear, aware, loving, creative consciousness. Be with this awareness for a while.'

I look round the room and feel a deep calm as I see twelve relaxed people, breathing steadily, eyes closed, letting themselves be themselves. Margaret is smiling, a Buddha-like smile. Wolfgang still looks tense, sitting very straight in his chair. Sarah looks sad.

'When you are ready, slowly become aware of walking, walking along a country road. Take time to look around. Notice what the road is like. Is it straight or winding? What is the road made of? Look at the landscape, the fields, the trees. Become aware of the weather. Is it sunny? Windy? Be aware of what you are wearing. You walk on. How does it feel? Write down any important things that you want to remember.'

Several people take the opportunity to write something. Paul writes and writes; I wait for him for a minute, then decide to go on anyway.

'As you walk on, you become aware of a small figure in the distance, walking towards you. As you draw closer, you can see that it's a child, about five years old, and as you come closer still, you realize that this is you when you were five years old. When you come level with each other, you stop to greet one another. Notice what the child is wearing, the expression on its face, look and see if it is carrying anything. Notice how you greet each other.'

I pause for a moment for everyone to experience the meeting fully. I can hear David, sitting on the floor next to me, breathing short shallow breaths.

'The child has something to say to you. Listen carefully to what it has to say, how it says it. If you want to, write down the child's message.'

I shut my eyes for a moment to see myself in shorts and a grey cardigan with Fair Isle edging, inquisitive, leaning forward out of a faded photograph. What did I want to know? What is he saying? Something like: 'I want to make sense of all this. I want to understand what's going on.' Someone is crying, here in the room in the present; I can feel the tears coming to my own eyes. Looking round, Sarah and Glenys are both crying; David has silent tears running down his cheeks. Nearly everybody spends some time writing.

I take them back to the road, have them say goodbye to the five-year-old, noticing how they say goodbye and how it feels. Then we walk on along the road, being aware of the landscape we are walking through. Another figure coming towards us, an older child, a gradual realization that this is our ten-year-old self. 'See the child in your mind's eye, notice what the child is wearing, notice how you react as you come up to each other.' Again the child wants to say something to us; we listen carefully, write down the message if we want to.

This meeting appears to be less painful. Sarah still looks very sad; Wolfgang hard and serious. Judith smiles, then laughs quietly. My ten-year-old self, when I close my eyes to see him, is shy and withdrawn, but desperately wants to please me. 'Notice me,' he says. He's holding out a very detailed model of a house with red brick walls and furniture inside made out of matchboxes. I took it to school, kept it in my desk because I was frightened of having it taken away. Nobody saw it; I wanted them to notice me. Anger.

Back to the road again, and a temporary farewell to another part of our childhood. The next encounter is with a teenager, our fifteen-year-old self, getting ready to leave school, become an adult. A long time ago for some of us, not so long for others. Listen. What does the fifteen-year-old want to tell us?

My fifteen-year-old is confused, apparently free and self-confident, yet at the same time frightened and lonely. 'I can manage,' he says. I shiver. I think I can hear something alongside the confidence, something like 'Help!' I write them both down. When I look round Paul is writing again; he turns the page. I think Anna's asleep, her mouth open, clenched fists resting on knees pressed tight together. I wonder what she's getting from the weekend. As I watch her, she jolts awake. 'If you need to, write down what your fifteen-year-old says to you,' I say again for Anna's benefit.

'When you are ready, go back to the road and say goodbye to the teenager. Watch carefully how you say goodbye, how you leave each other, how it feels. Start to walk again; become aware again of the road. Can you see where the road is going? Look around you at the landscape. What can you see? Be aware of yourself as you walk along the road, how you are walking, how it feels.'

I sense a calmness in the room again as each person concentrates on the experience of being themself, a traveller on the road.

'In your own time — there's no hurry at all — let the road and the landscape fade, open your eyes, and bring yourself back to this room, these people; back to the here and now.'

I lean back in my chair and stretch, and wait for everybody to arrive back from their travels.

'Good. Now, with these memories and feelings still near the surface, find somebody to work with that you haven't yet had much contact with, and sit with them just as we did yesterday in the counselling exercise.'

While they find their partners I put more wood on the fire, then sit on the hearthrug watching them. Paul is taking his time to choose again. I bet it won't be one of the men; he'll have to hurry though. Ah. Paul and Margaret this time. They come and sit near me.

'We'll take five minutes each to tell our partner the important things about our experiences from the meditation. Choose one of you to begin, and the other will give full attention until it's their turn.' Paul's forgotten his notes, and bustles over to fetch them. What's an experience without detailed notes? 'Start when you're ready.' I sit and listen to Margaret and Paul.

Paul begins. 'I found it very difficult to relax. I was busy last night organizing my work for next week. Silly really, but I couldn't get it out of my head this morning. It took me ages. But then I found the road; it was quite a twisty road between two high banks, like a country lane, hedges either side, tarmac underfoot. I couldn't see what I was wearing. I couldn't see very far ahead either, so when the young child appeared he wasn't far away. He looked surprised to see me, frightened, as though he wanted to run away.

He wasn't carrying anything. He tried . . . he tried to get past me without meeting me, but the road was too narrow for that. I said hello. The child turned away and said, "I don't want you." I felt quite upset, and I didn't know what to do. It reminded me of other children saying that to me and me being upset about that too.

'When I walked on I could feel it getting more difficult to walk, almost as though I was frightened of something coming round a bend in the road. I looked around and noticed that I could see over the banks — they'd got lower. On the left was quite a thick wood, a birch wood. On the right was a hedge and then a field with tall grass in it.

'My ten-year-old was quiet and reserved; I thought he was going to ignore me again, but he came up to me and said, "I want you to be my friend." I looked at him and felt very sad, but I reached out my arms and he came up, warily to begin with, and we hugged each other. I was sorry to say goodbye. He wanted me to stay and play with him, but we promised to see each other again.'

Paul smiles sadly and pauses, looks away.

'Go on,' says Margaret.

'Well, the road began to widen out then, with grass on both sides, like a big level plain, so I could see my fifteen-year-old a long way off. He seemed to be looking for something — I don't know what. He didn't say anything to me, though I listened. Perhaps he just said "Hi!" as he passed. I let him go, but I felt disappointed that he didn't say anything. Oh well. Then the road started going up a hill and I could see it winding up ahead of me. "Just keep going," I thought.

'That was about it. How about you?'

I look at my watch. Near enough to five minutes. 'Time to change.'

'My road went through fields,' says Margaret, 'open on both sides. Oh, sorry. I forgot to say about relaxing. It was good. Yes, I did feel very relaxed.

'The road. Yes, meadows on either side, lots of wild flowers. I stopped to pick them. Poppies, cornflowers. The child came and picked flowers with me. It was me in a blue and white check frock. We had a lovely time together. She said, "I like playing," and I said, "I do too." We laughed together, then she danced off with her bunch of flowers and waved. That was good.

'When I looked again there was a stream by the road. The road was more of a path really, a footpath like the one I used to walk to school along. The older child was sitting on a little bridge, on the brick wall. She was bored, but she was pleased that I'd come. She said, "Let's run," so we ran together a little way along the path. Then she said, "I've got to go now," and went back the way we'd come. Actually, no she didn't. Sorry. She more sort of disappeared. I can't remember.

'Then the path went on, I think past a cornfield. Yes, yellow corn. I took some and chewed it. I felt restless. I couldn't see the fifteen-year-old for a long time. I think I was trying too hard. Then she did come. She was very cross. She said, "Listen to me, listen to me," over and over, like that. She was wearing the yellow and orange skirt I used to wear to church. "Listen to me," she said. Mmmmm. Sorry.'

'You don't need to be sorry, Margaret,' says Paul. I smile. Margaret smiles too.

'Yes. You're right. Where was I?'

'The fifteen-year-old.'

'Yes. Well, she looked at me very seriously, and I cried. I felt sad. We said goodbye and waved for a long time. Then what? Well, the path started to curve round behind the cornfield, and I looked up and the sky was quite grey — it had been sunny. I thought it might be going to rain. Then John said to stop, so that was it.'

'Well done,' says Paul.

We remember past experiences in different ways. When most people talk about memory, they mean remembering with our mind, describing things from the past in words. This 'brain memory' is an important part of recalling our past experiences. However, there are other ways in which we store experience, ways which are not so commonly acknowledged, but which can be tapped just like our mental memory.

Our body can often remember experiences that our brain overlooks or puts to one side. We can delve into this 'body memory' just as we can into our mental memory, but since we use it less often, it sometimes needs a little practice before we can use it efficiently. Our mental memory is frequently nudged into action by an event or experience which recalls past events, and the same is true of our body memory. If somebody touches me in a certain way, for instance, my body will tend to respond in a similar way to earlier times when I was touched in that way. Sometimes our bodies can 'remember' past events better than our brains. The same is true of feelings; feeling a particular feeling in the present can remind us of previous times when we felt the same feeling, and our 'feeling memory' is often more efficient than our mental memory at recalling vividly a past event.

Using feelings and physical sensations in this way provides a useful technique for recalling the past when our mental memory is having problems in remembering the details of an event. As people start to explore their early memories, they often discover vitally important events which have been banished from their conscious memories until they begin to delve into their feelings and physical sensations. Re-remembering formative events is a vital and worthwhile exploration, and using feelings and sensations to aid our mental memories is one way to recover the past. There are others, too. One useful insight is that the more we go over a particular event or experience from our past, the more we shall remember. When we rediscover an important event, it often helps to tell it several times to somebody who is willing to listen and give us attention while we recount it — this, if you remember, is the technique I used with Wolfgang when he was remembering the incident with his sister and the model aeroplane.

Another technique is called scanning, and works best in a counselling situation where we can rely on full attention while we do it. Scanning means moving quickly from memory to memory, remembering as many details as we can connected with a particular part of our life. The memories may be of a certain period — everything we can remember from primary school, for instance. They could be memories connected with an important person — our mother, perhaps — or everything we can remember about our earliest sexual experiences. Once we start scanning our memory, especially if we use our body and feeling memories alongside our brain memory, we shall almost certainly find that the detail we are able to recall is far beyond what we originally imagined to be possible.

This is particularly true where the experiences we are recalling are painful ones. Memories of joy and excitement, times when we experienced the flow of love, are usually relatively easy to remember. Painful times when our power and intelligence were denied, times when our love was being blocked, are often more difficult to remember, and crucial formative experiences which hurt us deeply can sometimes be completely 'forgotten'. In order to protect ourselves we are able to put such memories out of our easy-access mental memory, but they don't go away that easily, and our body will remember them even when our mind denies their existence.

Another aid to recalling formative experiences is to allow fantasy and dream a place in the recovery of the past. We have a tendency to trust our mental memory because it seems reliable and accurate — the recalling in words of the detail of an event appears to validate and legitimize the memory better than 'vague' feelings and fantasies. Detailed mental memory is certainly important, but especially when we go back into our early childhood, or try to discover where we first learnt to block our love, our brain memory on its own is sometimes of limited value — we can recall certain incidents, but no matter how hard we try we can't remember anything else.

It is here that exercises like the one we have just done can be extremely useful. By using our imagination to give us hooks to hang memories on — imagining ourselves as a child, letting the child speak, noticing its reactions to us as adults — we can recall in a very direct and immediate way part of the experience of being the child. As long as we are not consciously fabricating the past or deliberately lying, we don't need to be particularly concerned with accuracy as we remember our early experiences. Just because we can't remember the details of a childhood trauma, it doesn't make it any less traumatic. A feeling that something happened is quite sufficient to suggest that it, or something like it, did happen, and the more painful the experience, the more likely it is that we have protected ourself against the pain by 'forgetting' the detail of the experience. Therefore it's all the more important to trust our imagination, our fantasies and our dreams, even when our heavily-conditioned mental memory suggests that our imagination is at fault.

When Sigmund Freud was interviewing women for his work on

hysteria, so many of them described 'vague fantasies' about being sexually molested by their fathers that he suggested, at least in his early work, that all women have a subconscious desire to be incestuously sexual. Because of his cultural upbringing, Freud had to believe that respectable fathers don't interfere with their daughters, and therefore that these women's imaginings were pure fantasy and had no basis in truth. What we now know about the incidence of father/daughter incest and Victorian attitudes towards sexuality suggests that the events being described by Freud's interviewees were memories of actual experiences, and had little or nothing to do with the children's subconscious desires.

Fantasy memory, dream memory, and the imaginary reconstruction of past events, can all be extremely important tools in the exploration of our past. Recovering our past, especially the events and experiences which blocked the flow of love and led us to protect ourselves unnecessarily, is essential if we are to understand who we are and how we came to be this way. Until we begin to deal with the pain and distress from the past which haunt our behaviour, we are doomed to react in the same rigid, patterned ways whenever somebody or something reminds us of past events which we can so easily believe are lost beyond recall. They are not: memory is a wonderful phenomenon, and the integration of mind, body and imagination into a trusted structure for recalling the details, the thoughts and the feelings of past events is immensely liberating.

Chapter Nine

Women and Men

After sitting for so long we need to move. We play a very simple game, one that I learnt at primary school — hug tag. One person is 'it', and 'it' has to catch people who aren't locked in an embrace. But you can only hug up to a count of three, then you're on your own again. It raises the pulse, the blood-pressure, and the noise level, and it gets people back into contact with each other. After ten minutes of hug tag I tell the group that we'll have a fifteen-minute break.

Judith and I talk about the next part of the workshop over a cup of coffee at the kitchen table. I have asked her if she will lead the women's group when we divide after the break, and I explain the outline of what we shall be doing. We shall be using all the techniques we have learnt to explore our pasts, especially our histories as women and men. We shall be remembering times when we were told that we had to be certain ways because of our gender, and times when we were limited in our actions and choices because of our gender. For anybody that has taken part in a consciousness-raising group, this will be nothing new.

Then we shall move from the past into the present, and I suggest to Judith that we give each group the opportunity to think about three questions to do with communication between the two groups, between men and women. I've written them down:

— What do you want everybody in the other group to hear about your experiences as a woman or as a man?
— What do you want everybody in the other group to promise never again to do to you as a woman or as a man?
— What support do you need from the people in the other group

to help you to acknowledge your personal power as a woman or as a man?

'Isn't that too complicated?' asks Judith. 'Can't we just ask what the women want the men to hear and vice versa?'

I laugh. 'I'm so glad you're here, Judith. You're right. You might find it useful to have the three questions in your mind, but yes, the simpler the better.'

Ray, David, Maurice, Paul, Wolfgang and I sit in a circle by the window. The women are sitting at the other end of the room, round the fire. The rain has stopped and a dull sun can just be made out through the clouds. We sit close to each other, and the first thing we do is to hold hands and close our eyes for a minute or so, to bring ourselves fully to the new group, to let go of what has gone before and prepare ourselves for the next experience.

We start with the very earliest things we can remember — lying in a pram watching kites flying, losing a toy car in a sand dune, falling downstairs on a tricycle, David cutting his own hair, discovering the freedom of experiment and the puzzlement of adult reaction, lions at the zoo through railings, a new baby and a father saying 'That's your new brother', attendant feelings of pride and anger.

Earliest sexual memories next, memories guaranteed to help us contact our feelings about being men, aware of being men. Memories of being expected to know what to do and being scared which make Ray shiver. Memories of being laughed at by other boys which bring up anger for David.

'I find it very difficult to talk about my earliest sexual memory,' says Maurice, 'because it brings up a lot of stuff about boarding school. I feel angry already. I was in bed the night after I arrived; I must have been twelve. I was nearly asleep, and I felt somebody getting into my bed. I looked around and it was a boy called Charles. I can't remember much about it, but I know he put his hand inside my pyjama trousers and held my penis and rubbed it. A very confused mixture of being very scared, enjoying the sensation, and knowing that it was wrong, very wrong. I didn't know what to do. I lay very still indeed. I think he must have asked me to do it to him, and I couldn't. I just couldn't touch him there. He said something like "If you don't do it to me, I'll . . ." — can't remember what. It was very threatening. He went, and though I was very relieved, I couldn't sleep all night, worrying, worrying.' Maurice lowers his head and closes his eyes for a moment, then looks up. 'And I'm sure that's why I don't trust the friendship of men. I don't know what they want when they come close. I mean it's fine if it's David, for instance, but men. Ugghh.'

'Maurice? What would you need to do to affirm your friendship and closeness with these men — with Paul and Ray and Wolfgang and me?'

'I could smile at you all. No, I'd need . . . I want to know . . . I want to know that it's safe to be close, physically close. I want to know what you want from me.'

'How would it be if each of us hugged you and said, "I love you, Maurice, and I don't want anything from you"?'

'Oh god,' says Maurice, smiling and shivering at the same time. 'Can I handle that?'

'Can you?'

Maurice handles it very well. At the end, with David's arm round him and Wolfgang holding his hand, he says: 'I must do that more often.'

Wolfgang remembers watching a class of girls changing for swimming, and feeling very excited. Paul tells us about his sexual relationship with his mother before he was born; I find it hard to concentrate, and yawn to stay present. My memory is of reading *Titbits* and *Health and Efficiency* when I stayed with my grandparents who ran a newsagents, lying in bed stroking myself and wondering why the people in the retouched photographs had no genitals. I liked the breasts though.

'I've just remembered something else,' says David. 'I don't think I've ever told anyone else — I've only just remembered it myself — but it feels important. When I was about eleven or twelve, I took some girls' clothes — I think it was just a pair of tight pants and a skirt, the sort with an elastic waist — from some jumble-sale clothes my mother was organizing. I hid them in my room, and several times, late at night, I got up and put them on. I remember it felt so good.' David laughs nervously. 'I just loved the combination of the tightness and the loose material of the skirt. One night I let myself out of the house wearing them, and went to play on the swings in the playground next door. It was scary — what if anyone saw me? — but so exciting. Then the clothes just disappeared from under my bed; my parents never said anything. Now I feel embarrassed, but it did feel very good wearing those clothes.' David pauses. 'Sometimes in the evening I wear one of Gina's long skirts,' he shuts his eyes and smiles. 'Same feeling. Nice.'

Paul is looking at David very strangely, frowning. I take Paul's hand and feel — I think — a wince before he relaxes.

'Let's take some time to talk about when we felt limited by being boys,' I say. 'David's already started — boys don't wear skirts. What are some times when we wanted to do things but weren't allowed because we were boys?'

Memories of being told not to play with a sister's dolls' house, of sometimes wanting to be the mummy in 'mothers and fathers', of being told not to cry because boys don't, of being hit when the girls weren't.

Paul wants to say something. 'I know we do learn a lot about being boys, and how boys are certain ways and girls other ways,' he says, 'but of course it's important to remember that because we're male there are ways that we can't be. I mean, women are just built to have babies and feed them. The mothering instinct is very important, and men just can't do it. When we were hunter-gatherers and the women had to stay at home and look after the babies, the men had to go and get food, and that meant hunting it, and it meant that they had to be strong and brave, and so we have to be very careful when it comes to limitations, because we *are* limited, and . . .'

'Hang on,' says David, sitting up on his knees. 'You've made at least six questionable assumptions already. Men can't nurture, you say. Men can't give love to babies. Women have to stay at home. Women don't have to be brave. Who are you limiting?'

'But we're all limited like that,' says Paul, his voice rising. 'Men can't choose to be pregnant. They don't have the babies so they don't have that basic instinct, that bond.'

'Oh, bonds,' says David. 'Bonds like dependence and "mummy's always there" and tied to the kitchen. Great.'

'This is turning into an argument,' I say. 'Is that what we want?'

'But that's the way it *is*,' says Paul, ignoring me and leaning forward towards David. 'Women just are different. Complementary of course, yin and yang, animus and anima, but women have the passive nurturing qualities and men are, well, more active, out there. You can see it all the time. Nurture is what women have to give. It's obvious.'

I have been aware for a few minutes of somebody in the women's group crying, have tried not to let it take my attention from Paul and David. Suddenly the crying rises to a scream, a long shrill scream which echoes round the room. My forehead tingles. Paul talks on, over the scream; Ray and Wolfgang strain forward to hear him. 'And men have other things to give, so it's not that we're unequal.' David has shut his eyes and crossed his arms over his chest. 'I wouldn't for a moment suggest that that makes us unequal,' continues Paul as the scream ends, 'but it does make it immmmmmmm . . .'

I have reached out to Paul, put one hand behind his head and the other over his mouth. 'Keep trying to talk, Paul.'

'Mmmmmmmmmm,' says Paul, pushing at my arms.

'A woman screamed,' I say to Paul quietly. He stops struggling and looks at me. 'A woman screamed, Paul.' Paul's mouth is open, as though he wants to say something, but he remains silent.

'What's the feeling, Paul?'

Paul shivers. He is silent for maybe half a minute, then looks up and speaks. 'For a moment I was really angry,' he says, 'but stopping talking uncovered something else. When you said what you said — a woman screamed — I suddenly felt quite numb, like a jolt.' He shivers again. 'Yes, shivers up my spine. Ugh.'

'And the thought?'

'The thought? I don't want to know. Walk away. Someone else will deal with it.'

David still has his eyes shut. 'David?'

'It's okay,' says David, opening his eyes and nodding slowly. 'I'm okay.'

'Do you want to say anything about that experience?'

'I'm confused. The feeling is anger and frustration, but I don't know whether it's to do with Paul or the scream. Probably both.'

'Which do you want to deal with first?'

David laughs. 'Paul?'

I pass him a cushion. 'Okay.' I turn to Paul: 'Paul, remember the anger is David's anger; you are not to blame for David's anger. If you need to feel your feelings when he's felt his, we'll deal with them then.' Paul looks worried, but nods. 'Anger and frustration, David. How are you going to express it?'

David expresses it by thumping the cushion and breathing out hard as he thumps. 'Ooooh! Ooooh! Ooooh!'

'Are there words that go with that, David?'

'Listen!' shouts David. 'Yes. Listen! Listen! Listen!' He thumps the words home. 'Listen! Listen! Another thought though: Stop it! Stop! Stop! Stop! Stop! Owwwww! I banged my hand on the floor. Stop.'

'Keep going, David.'

'Oh, stop. Stop. Stop. Ohhh.'

'Who are you saying that to, David?'

'Gina. Stop, Gina. I'm on to the scream now. Gina screams. Oh, stop. Please stop.'

'The feeling?'

'Helpless, I don't know what to do. Oh, please stop. I'm stuck. I don't know what to do. She's out of control. She'll break something. She'll hurt me. Oh.' David cowers, his hands over his face; cowers and shivers. I take his hands and give one to Paul to hold. 'David?'

No response.

'David? Are you there, David?'

'I'm thinking about Gina, feeling sad. Can't cry. Don't like it; don't like feeling sorry for myself.'

'Try saying, "It's great that people can feel their feelings." '

David says it several times, looks at me to say it again. Now the tears come, and Paul and I hold his hands and we all give him attention while he cries.

The sun breaks through at last, the tall rectangles of sunlight from the window creeping slowly across the floor. Next we look at the difficulties we have in being men.

Ray starts: 'I don't like the way women depend on men for money. I'd like to *not* think about earning money for other people. I'd like it if everyone got paid just for being alive so that money didn't mess up relationships.'

'I want to be with babies and children,' says David, 'and for that to be okay, especially with women — mothers. I want them to know that I'm good at it and can be trusted. I don't like the way a lot of women assume that I'm going to be useless and get things wrong.'

'I feel left out somehow,' says Wolfgang. 'I don't like women leaving me out of things.'

'Erections,' says Paul. 'I don't like having erections when I don't want them, and women getting frightened by them.'

'What I said about being useless and getting things wrong,' says David, 'it's really difficult. I don't like *not* knowing what to do and not wanting to ask a woman how to do it. But then, perhaps I do know what to do. But I'm frightened that she'll do it differently, or better, or something, and I'm going to be wrong. Oh dear, it's the pattern of not being able to be wrong. It doesn't matter if I get it wrong to begin with; it's more important to do it. I *can* make mistakes.'

Paul has been trying to interrupt David. 'Yes, we have problems too,' he says. 'We listen and listen to women, but they've got to accept that we have problems too. Men are just as oppressed as women are.'

'Oh Paul,' says David. 'Grrrrr.'

There is so much to say and do about relationships between women and men because there are so many things that could be so much better. The dynamic between David and Paul reminds me of many discussions and thoughts and feelings about the everyday practice of unconditional love. And questions. Who gives emotional support to whom? What is support, anyway? What is oppression, and who is oppressed? Is oppression a fact or a feeling? How can we conceive of equality when our circumstances are clearly so unequal?

Support first. In terms of a radical approach to love, support means validating a person's power and creativity, and helping them to deal with the blocks to their powerful loving nature. Easy words, but the current irrationality of most human relating makes the practice seem virtually impossible. The ways in which women and men can support each other's love and power are limitless, and in order to see clearly the ways in which this can be done we need to overcome all the limiting things we have learnt about our roles as men and women, mothers and fathers, sisters and brothers. With the great weight of convention and social limitation bearing down on us all the time, we have to be extremely courageous to believe that love does work, and that women and men do have the capacity to relate to each other as important, equal, powerful and independent human beings.

Part of this learning process is to examine very carefully the assumptions about relating that we have been taught, by exploring our own and other people's actual experiences, and comparing them with what we have been told about the ways in which human beings must or should relate. This is an enormous and fascinating area which has vast implications for our daily lives; for now I want to look at just one such assumption, Paul's belief that part of a woman's natural role is to nurture.

There is no question that it is part of our loving and caring nature to nurture each other, but the deep belief that men don't have feelings, and certainly don't have feelings of tenderness or sympathy, makes it very difficult for men to acknowledge any shared emotional life. The only emotional support that most men receive comes first from their mothers and then from their wives. The idea of men crying on each other's shoulders or telling each other the details of their personal lives is quite beyond the average man's imagination.

When things go wrong for little boys, mummy is the one person who can usually be guaranteed to provide the comfort and warmth that help to heal the hurt. But there comes a time when being big and strong means that we cut off the comfort and push the feelings underground until we can find a mummy-substitute for our emotional support (and usually an enormous and unjustified amount of practical support too), and when they have found her, many men marry her to ensure the continuation of the service.

On the other hand, girls continue to go to mummy for comfort, and thereafter women receive most of their emotional support from other women, who share the same experiences and can understand and sympathize. Women would often like to have emotional and practical support from men, but most women experience very little such support and have come not to expect it. The vital exchange and closeness between women which provides them with everyday support is exactly what most men miss; when a man sees women enjoying close time together, the feelings (unacknowledged of course, since this is a man) are often, as Wolfgang describes, jealousy and rejection. A typical male reaction is then to belittle the contact between the women by labelling it as gossip.

Yet this is exactly the sort of emotional support that men need, and for which they usually turn to women. Not surprisingly, as women become aware that they are providing the emotional support for the entire population, many are rebelling against the expectation that women will do all of the emotional work in our society. Paula Jennings, in a booklet called *Love Your Enemy?*, is very clear that, 'Men must learn to nurture each other, and if they can't then I don't believe they will survive.' I think that at last things are beginning to change as a few men glimpse what support and comfort and warmth men can give each other, but generations of conditioning work against the process. As men, we have to be in touch with our feelings and share them with each other; we have to learn how to be warm, supportive and nurturing to other people — men, women and children, and since men nurturing men is the least practised art, it is the one that needs the most attention, as Ray, Wolfgang, David, Maurice, Paul and I are learning.

It's not easy to see exactly what oppression is. It certainly exists as a reality of social behaviour, and at the same time feeling oppressed, when we can sort out what that actually feels like, seems to be a very personal experience. I am going to define the social reality of oppression in a way that fits into my radical theory of love: oppression is the widespread and systematic invalidation, both in beliefs and in actions, of the power and intelligence of one distinguishable group of people by another, to which end the oppressor group frequently maintains power over the oppressed group through laws, conventions and institutions, and an inflexible belief that they are right and justified in their actions.

Oppression is clearly at work whenever anybody believes themself to be better than another person by virtue of their membership of a selfstyled 'superior' group. Obvious oppressions are the oppression of black people by whites, minorities by majorities, poor people by rich people, and women by men. Less obvious oppressions include the oppression of physically handicapped people in an environment designed only for the able-bodied, the oppression of children in an adult-centred world, and the oppression of people who live on their own in a society where 'the family' is the norm. Oppression is often described in terms of the nature of the oppression — sexism, classism, racism or agism.

Using this definition of oppression, I have to disagree with Paul. Men oppress women, women are oppressed by men. To say that men are oppressed by women not only invalidates the reality of women's experience, it also conveniently ignores who it is that is actually limiting men — my belief is that it is almost invariably other men. Men can be oppressed in other ways, by being poor, handicapped or black; they are not oppressed as men. But I am not denying Paul's feelings if he says he *feels* oppressed as a man. I think three things are happening here. The first is that, as we have seen, feelings are no reliable guide to rational behaviour, and feelings do not necessarily indicate truths. Secondly, if Paul says 'I'm feeling oppressed' it is difficult for him to own the feeling, because it implies that somebody is doing the oppressing. Where oppression is at work, of course, somebody *is* doing the oppressing, but it's important to separate the feelings from the facts. Thirdly, 'oppression' can often be a misleading label for a feeling. Because oppression is a reality of social behaviour, it's more useful to acknowledge that fact and go beyond 'feeling oppressed' to explore those feelings more immediately. Beyond the feeling of oppression lurk anger, frustration, sadness, which all need to be felt and cleared if the reality of oppression is to be tackled effectively.

When we feel bad, as we saw in Chapter Six, it's very easy to blame other people for our bad feelings. This happens a great deal around the phenomenon of oppression, because it seems so clear that the oppressors are to blame for the plight of the oppressed. Here, almost more than anywhere else, we need to remember the uselessness of blame if we want things to change. It's so easy when you *know* you are being oppressed to feel bad, and to tell the person who has triggered the feelings that they *are* oppressive and that they *are* sexist. It may well be true — oppression is real and people are oppressive — but the situation is unlikely to change until the oppressors themselves understand the futility of oppression in the face of personal love and power. It's certainly worth telling someone that you think they are being oppressive *if* they are able to hear you, and one of the first things that someone from an oppressor group can do if they want to challenge oppression is to take seriously what an oppressed person is saying about them, even if they can't understand or agree with what is being said. But beware of devaluing important insights like oppression and sexism by using them like an all-purpose battering ram to hit people with, and avoid offloading your bad feelings onto the person who triggered them with an indiscriminate 'that was really oppressive', or 'how sexist'.

The systematic invalidation of one group of people by another is a denial of human intelligence on a vast scale, yet it is frequently compounded by the difficulty experienced by the person who is being oppressed to recognize that their limiting patterns are the result of oppression. A woman may have been told uncountable times that she was no good at maths — this is invalidation taking the form of sexism in education, a denial of the woman's intelligence. She has heard it so often that she has completely come to believe it; she knows that figures frighten her, she relates it to other women's experience and the popular myth of the feather-brained woman. She tells herself: that's just the way it is — women are useless at maths and I'm no exception. Here the oppression has been internalized — the person who has been invalidated believes that the invalidation represents nothing less than the truth, and that there is no alternative to the fear and helplessness she feels around the aspect of her life that has been invalidated. Thus the institutionalized denial of power becomes not only part of the world view of those who believe that they have a right to oppress; it also becomes incorporated into the belief system of oppressed people.

Nobody deserves to be helpless, however, and except in extreme cases of the violation of human rights, nobody is helpless. Oppression, and especially internalized oppression, is an enormous block to the acknowledgement of personal love, intelligence and power, but blocks can be dealt with. By feeling fully the feelings of fear and helplessness, and discovering the power to act and change, we can break out of even the deepest doubt and despair.

People who argue for the normality of a pecking order in society, who try to convince us that a hierarchy of power is good for us, frequently invoke supposedly 'normal' differences between groups of people to explain inequalities in people's personal circumstances. 'Single mothers can't expect to provide children with the same things as a family,' they say. 'The working classes wouldn't appreciate the sort of education we give the upper classes.' 'Blacks like living on top of each other, it reminds them of home.' People's circumstances are different, and their access to resources and support is vastly unequal. But this is not because people are unequal; it's because those who choose to maintain power over others will not acknowledge and act upon the principle of the equality of human beings. People are equal; their circumstances are far from equal.

To match a basic belief in equality with a reality of equal opportunity requires action from both oppressed and oppressor. It requires people who are oppressed to deal with their feelings of helplessness and discover their power, and it requires those who have power over others to relinquish that power and deal with their feelings of vulnerability. This 'power over' — this privilege — takes many forms, from physical force to a subtle pressure to conform to the oppressor's wishes and beliefs.

Internalized oppression and the difficulty of letting go of privilege were well illustrated at lunchtime yesterday. When Glenys fetched the cloth and bent down to clear up Wolfgang's food she may have been doing it out of a genuine desire to support Wolfgang, but the chances are that Wolfgang's predicament and neediness triggered a pattern in Glenys based on a belief that women always clear up when men have domestic accidents. It would not be too improbable to imagine that when she was younger Glenys was frequently expected to clear up other people's messes. The original invalidation was to expect her to do it even when she didn't want to, even when the mess had been made by someone who could clear it up just as well as her. Over the years the invalidation has become internalized, until Glenys's immediate reaction to a minor accident is to clear it up without question.

And Wolfgang lets her, feels even as he picks up the soggy lettuce that it's not for him to clear it up, that if he looks helpless for long enough a mummy figure will come up and let him off. His privilege is the other side of Glenys's oppression — the patterns lock together and perpetuate a rigid way of relating which denies equality and intelligence. What a good thing Judith was there to interrupt both patterns simultaneously with a well-timed expletive.

And what do we like about being men?

Wolfgang likes his strength. Maurice likes his dependability and reliability. Paul likes his penis. David laughs and Paul looks at him suspiciously. David says: 'I like the way we can love each other and laugh at each other's patterns.' Ray likes his neatness and skill with wood. I like the way I am learning to listen to people telling me about how they experience me as a man.

Remembering that we can be pleased with ourselves and take pride in ourselves without needing to be better or more privileged than other people, we take it in turn to stand up and take pride in being a man. Ray goes first and I stand beside him with an arm round his waist as he says: 'I'm proud to be a man.' Then it's Ray's turn to support David, and so on until we are all able to look our brothers in the eyes and tell them how pleased we are to be men.

As I sit down after my turn, David shivers and says, 'Phew. Yes, that's what it's all about. Loving ourselves. I wish I could believe it all the time.'

'I need to move,' says Maurice. 'Somebody come and dance with me.' Before I have time to think we are all on our feet, arms linked in a chain, dancing with Maurice leading us. I feel stupid to begin with, then get into it, weaving round the room, jumping up and down. 'Proud to be men', sings Maurice, 'proud to be men.' I start giggling, feel as though I want to say, 'Don't get carried away,' but Maurice sings on. I'm aware of the women watching us. I'm feeling embarrassed and I think they must be too — projection. 'Proud to be men,' sings Maurice, and links up with Paul at the other end of the chain.

'Enough!' I shout. I can't handle it any longer. We stop singing and fall together in a group hug, breathless. I think we've got the idea. Somebody at the other end of the room starts clapping and all the other women join in.

I disentangle myself from the hug, check with Judith that the women have completed their group process, and announce a five-minute break.

★ ★ ★

Judith and I prepare the room and compare our experiences in the groups. We set two lines of chairs facing each other down the length of the room, six on one side for the women and five on the other for the men, and a blackboard and easel near the window.

'It was a good group,' says Judith. 'Very clear, and very aware. Anna was quiet though, I wish she'd say something. There's a lot going on for her but she won't let it out.' I tell Judith briefly about the men and how we never got round to the three questions, by which time people are drifting back. I direct them to their appropriate chairs.

'Up until lunch we're going to take time to listen carefully to each other as women and men. We shall pay attention to what the people in the other group want to say to us. It may be things they want us to know about them, it may be things they want to tell us about the way they see us behaving or the ways in which they would like us to change. Clear statements and attentive listening. Judith will write everything down so we can remember the important things that are said.

'We'll start with the women, since women frequently have to listen to men first. What do you, as women, want to say to the men in the group?'

There is a long pause while several of the women look at each other, then Glenys puts up her hand and starts. 'I want you all to know that sex frightens me. I've had a lot of bad experiences with men and sex, and it's made me so scared that I don't much want to be close to men, at least not physically. And I'm sad about that, because I do know some quite nice men.' Glenys stops and looks down; Penny, sitting next to her, takes her hand. Glenys looks up at her, then continues. 'So I want you to understand my fear and where it comes from, and I want you to respect my fear when you relate to me.'

'Well done, Glenys. That was courageous. Can you say the same thing in one sentence, and look at all the men as you say it to make sure they are listening?'

Glenys nods. 'I'm afraid of being sexual with men, and I want you to respect my fear,' she says, looking along the row of men. Judith writes it down.

'I'll go next,' says Sarah, 'because mine's connected with Glenys's. I want to show my physical desire sometimes, but I want *me* to decide how the closeness progresses. I don't want to be taken over.'

As the list progresses each woman says at least one thing which she wants the men to hear. Eventually none of them wants to say anything else for now, and the list reads:

— I am afraid of being sexual with men, and I want you to respect my fear. (Glenys)
— I want to show my desire sometimes, but I want me to decide how the closeness progresses. (Sarah)
— Don't be afraid of showing how sensitive and tender you are. (Margaret)
— I want you to respect me as a whole human being, not as a physical object. (Judith)
— I want you to be my friends and not always something more. I want to be able to be with a man like I can be with a woman. (Sarah)
— I want you to help me or go away. I want you to know what to do without always asking. (Penny)
— If you persist in needing to look after me or needing me to look after you, you're never going to learn to look after each other. (Judith)
— I want to see men joyful, not suffering. (Ursula)
— I'm not blaming you, I just want you to change. (Anna)
— Give me back my power: hand it over peacefully, I don't want to fight. (Penny)
— Let me love you as equal to equal. (Margaret)

After the women comes the turn of the men. Paul starts: 'I want to say how beautiful you are,' he says to the women.

'Great,' I say. 'Why don't you? Look at each woman in turn, say her name, and tell her how beautiful she is.'

Paul looks slightly startled, but soon gets into it. 'Glenys, you are beautiful. Penny, you are beautiful.' As he goes along the line I watch the women's different reactions — Glenys's nervous smile, Penny's openness, Anna's impassivity. Judith writes down 'You are beautiful. (Paul)'.

'I like your company,' says David, 'and I don't need anything from you.'

As the men talk to the women, Judith writes everything down.
— You are beautiful. (Paul)
— I like your company, and I don't need anything from you. (David)
— I want you to love the child in me. (Paul)
— Thank you for everything you have taught us. (Maurice)
— I want to listen to your experiences of men, including me, without being protective or defensive. (John)
— I like my sensitivity and tenderness. (Ray)
— I want you to respect that I am trying hard to be sensitive. (Paul)
— I love being with children and babies, and I would like you to trust me with the children you look after. (David)
— Please accept me with my fears and insecurities. (Wolfgang)
— I want to understand your experience as women. (David)

As Paul starts speaking for the fourth time I sense an uneasiness in the room. 'I want you to accept my spiritual integrity,' he says, leaning forward in his chair and looking along the line of women as he speaks.

'Can I say something?' asks Judith. She checks with each person, and when she has agreement to continue she says, 'Paul, I wonder if you're aware that you keep asking for things from us as women. You want us to love you, you want us to respect you and accept you. You want, you want. But what are you going to *give*, Paul?'

Paul looks lost. Judith goes up to him, kneels in front of him and takes his hands. 'What are you going to give, Paul?' Paul is staring at Judith, his lips tight together, his breathing shallow and irregular.

I move behind him, put my arms round his stomach and squeeze. 'Express that feeling, Paul. Make the noise. Let go of the block.' I can feel his body tense and rigid. Everybody's attention is on him.

Paul explodes.

He opens his mouth and yells. He yells for maybe twenty seconds, struggles for breath, yells again, falters. All the time Judith gives him undivided attention, continues to hold his hands. Paul groans: 'Oh. Oh. Oh. Oh. Ohhhh.'

'Well done, Paul,' says Judith, looking into his eyes. 'What are you going to give?'

Paul starts to nod slowly. 'Yes,' he says. 'You're right. Thank you,

Judith. I'll think seriously about it and tell you when I've thought.'
Judith squeezes his hands, goes back to the blackboard and writes:
'I shall think seriously about what I can give. (Paul)'.

'One more before we stop for lunch,' I say, 'but that's no reason
to stop thinking about these things for the rest of our lives.'

David is last. He looks slowly at the line of women. 'I'm ready
to change,' he says. 'I want to say it to each of you, to help me
remember and to tell you individually about my intention.' He goes
back to the end of the row. 'Glenys, I am ready to change. Penny,
I'm ready to change. Anna, I'm ready to change. Margaret, I'm
ready to change. Sarah, I'm ready to change. Ursula, I'm ready
to change. Phew. I am, I'm ready to change.'

'Thank you David,' I say as Judith writes, 'I am ready to change.
(David)'. 'It's lunchtime, but before you go make sure you hug
everybody in the group.'

I need a break. I ignore my own instruction and the rest of the
group, and go for a long walk in the garden.

Chapter Ten

Taking Directions

After ten minutes my head has cleared and I can face them all again. I'm just about to sit down with my lunch when Anna comes over and says, 'Can I talk to you for a minute?'

'Yes, of course. Why don't you bring your lunch and we'll sit together?'

'Well actually,' says Anna, looking down, 'I'm not staying for lunch.' I put my plate down. 'No. I've enjoyed what we've been doing, but I've got an awful lot to do at home and a very busy day at the office tomorrow, so I think it's probably better if I get home and organize myself. But I do want to say thank you, and, well, it's been very good.'

I can feel a sinking feeling in my stomach, the feeling of failure tinged with impatience and annoyance.

I look at her for a moment. 'Anna, would you mind sitting down just while I say how I feel about that?' For a split second she looks scared, but sits down briskly and waits for me to speak.

I tell her about my feelings of failure, of frustration; how I usually feel annoyed and impatient if someone walks out on me without finishing something I feel is important. As I talk, I'm aware of Anna looking up at me. When I finish I look at her too, and see that her face has opened up, her lips are slightly parted.

'Anna, when did you decide not to stay?'

'About ten minutes ago.'

'So you didn't plan to be at home organizing things this afternoon.'

'No.' She pauses. 'I got everything ready on Friday.'

'Do you want to tell me why you changed your mind and decided not to stay?'

Anna closes her eyes, nearly smiles, opens them again. 'Not really
. . . but I will. I was feeling left out because I didn't think anyone
wanted to hug me. Not really. Even Paul didn't notice that he hadn't
hugged me till the very end — so much for him thinking I'm beautiful.
And this morning I've felt as though I'm not getting anywhere, not
dealing with any of the problems I need to deal with.'

'So how are you going to deal with them? By going home to
organize your life?'

Anna looks at me, breathes sharply, and puts her thumb behind
her top teeth. 'You think I should stay, don't you?'

'What do you want me to say, Anna? Only you know what you
want to do. I'd like you to stay, because I like having you in the
group.'

She nods. 'All right, you win.'

I laugh. 'How about rephrasing that?' I ask.

Anna laughs too. 'Okay, I win, but I wouldn't mind really getting
somewhere this afternoon. What are we going to do?'

'Choices, decisions and directions,' I say, taking my first mouthful
of lukewarm spaghetti.

We start the afternoon with a few seconds' silence, holding hands
with our eyes closed, then move straight into a game, though
perhaps 'Rain' would be better described as an exercise in group
creativity and imagination.

'We're going to make a rainstorm,' I say, 'and all you need to
do is follow my actions, and change them when I change mine.
Imagine that you're out for a walk — in the country or in a park.
It's a bright day, but overcast, like today. A fine rain begins to fall.'
I start to tap my two first fingers together and everybody follows
— the irregular tapping has an effect on the ear of light rain falling
on grass and trees. 'Soon it starts to get heavier' — two fingers
of each hand clapped together — 'and before long it's definitely
raining' — we all clap our hands to imitate the splash of raindrops
in puddles. 'Hmm, it's not just raining, this is going to be quite
a downpour' — hands thumped against chests — 'in fact, a real
drencher' — feet stamped on the wooden floor.

'It doesn't last long though, this sort of rain never does,' so gradually we revert to chest-thumping, clapping, two fingers and then one finger of each hand again. 'And now the rain is stopping, but there's still the drip of water from the leaves of the trees.' The single fingers tapped together slow down and gradually peter out. 'And the sun comes out again on a bright green well-washed world.'

'Okay. This afternoon's theme is relating what we have learnt so far this weekend to our everyday lives. We all have lives out there, and somehow we have to work out how to take the love we've experienced in this group into the world with us. We have jobs and friends and lovers and children; we have to make decisions about education and health, money and housing, how to spend our time, who to relate to and how.

'So how do all these practical everyday decisions and choices fit in with what we've learnt? I'm going to recap the main points we've come up with in the last day and a half, and then we'll spend some time working in pairs to see how the theory and practice of what we've been doing relates to our own lives. Stop me if you have any questions.

'Each of us is individually important; we are responsible for ourselves and we can take our lives in our own hands. We are powerful, despite everything we have ever learnt about being powerless.

'When we use our intelligence and power, and act in the knowledge of love, we can always respond to situations flexibly and creatively. This will frequently involve feeling and expressing the feelings that block our intelligence and power and love, but if we deal with the blocks, what follows is a clear flow of creative thought and action from which we can always find appropriate solutions.'

'Do you mean there's *always* a solution?' asks Ray. 'A solution to poverty and hunger and war?'

'Yes,' I say, then stop to feel the implications of my answer, a sudden tenseness high in my chest. 'Yes. What's the alternative? To believe that there isn't a solution?' Ray purses his lips and nods.

'And we always have choices; we are presented with choices all the time. Choice goes hand in hand with power; both are taken away and denied by oppressive practices, but a faith in the reality of limitless love and intelligence will always overcome powerlessness.'

'But choice doesn't always help a situation,' says Sarah. 'It can just be confusing. If I go into a shop and there's just a few things to choose from it's much easier than going into Sainsbury's or Marks and Spencers.'

'Mmm, I think the confusion is a feeling,' I say. 'Important to deal with, but a feeling. The question is, do you get what you want as often if your choice is limited? I think that very often a large range of choices feels confusing, but when the fear and insecurity are dealt with, it's very liberating to have a wide range of options, and you stand a much better chance of getting what you want. The connection between choice and confusion is an important one though.

'Choice. Yes, choice involves decisions and action. If we are going to contradict powerlessness and affirm our love and intelligence, we can't not choose. We have to choose all the time, otherwise we get stuck in rigid ways of reacting. And we have to act. It's all very well making decisions, but we have to act on them for anything to happen.

'And decisions and actions lead to change. Taking personal power, empowering other people and being active in the world, all help to make the world a better, more humane, beautiful and loving place.'

'Hear hear,' says Maurice.

Overcoming the legacy of powerlessness is much easier said than done; the weight of limitation is so heavy that the task often seems overwhelming. But we have to have faith in our power to change ourselves and the world, and a great deal of that empowerment comes from an understanding of how we came to be so powerless.

The more that we are expected to be a certain way, to conform to standards and stereotypes, the more we feel limited, trapped and tied down. We feel as though everybody and everything is forcing us to be a particular way and to play a particular role. We feel powerless to change anything, as though we have absolutely no choice other than to carry on in the same way day after day. And there is something safe and predictable, too, about the daily round. Even if we do feel trapped and tied down, we feel that it would be much harder to change things. In subtle ways we become addicted to our situation — trapped yet safe, limited yet predictable. We give our power and creativity away, and are supposedly content to be told what to do and how to be.

But if we give up our power and creativity, if we are persuaded that we are not a unique and important part of the flow of love, we give up the opportunity to choose our future. Yes, the pressures to conform are enormous; think what we would lose if we chose to do what *we* want to do instead of what other people want us to do. All that security and predictability would be at stake. But where our life is affected by decisions and choices, the most important opinion to take into account is our own. We can be sensitive to the thoughts and feelings of our friends, our partner, our parents or our children, but it's our life, and in the end any decisions affecting it must be ours.

In a society where so many people have such a great vested interest in keeping us powerless from infancy onwards, it's sometimes extremely difficult to remember that we can choose to live our own life, whatever the pressures to live it in the way that other people want. It's true, of course, that choice is often limited by circumstances — if I'm on social security I can't easily choose to buy a house or a new car; if I'm at home with the children I can't easily go out whenever I want; if I'm a black woman I can't easily get a half-decently paid job, if I can get one at all. But it's easy to believe, especially when we are being told so all the time, that because choice is limited we have no choice at all. 'I'm sorry,' we are told, 'you'll have to wait, you'll have to go without, you'll have to suffer. Only privilege will help you to bypass the queue.' The truth is that everybody, all the time, has choices — usually a wide range of choices. The challenge is to believe that creative change is always possible, and to deal with our own and other people's feelings about our choices. The results of taking our life in our own hands will undoubtedly upset the people who feel they have a right to tell us how to be. We can't afford to ignore their power or their feelings, especially when they are being critical or aggressive, but it is important to remember, and to carry on remembering, that the only person who knows what is best for me is me, and the only person who knows what is best for you is you.

★   ★   ★

On a sheet of paper pinned to the blackboard I have written:
— We can take responsibility for ourselves.
— We can respond creatively to any situation.
— We can always find appropriate solutions.
— We can always make choices for ourselves.
— We must choose and we must act.
— We can change ourselves and our world.
  (love works)

'Next we'll do an exercise designed to empower ourselves by clarifying what we want in our lives and the things we can do to achieve what we want.

'Harnessing the free flow of intelligence and creativity involves, as I've said, constant choice. Since every situation we find ourselves in is a new one, the most rational way of handling life is to be closely in touch with what we want all the time, making choices and decisions constantly, easily and lightly.

'That's often not very easy, because the society we live in is so rigid, and we have been bullied and frightened into believing either that we can't choose, or that many of the decisions we make are difficult and irrevocable. Neither of these is true. We can choose, *and* we can choose again, and again and again.

'Anna, I'd like it if you'd help me to demonstrate a way of getting in touch with our power to choose. Okay?' Anna smiles, and I set two cushions in the middle of the circle for us to sit on.

'This is called the what-do-you-want-and-how-can-you-get-it exercise. The idea is to work quickly and efficiently to assemble a range of aims and objectives, and then to think of ways of achieving those aims in detailed and specific ways. We work quickly to keep things light and creative and not get sunk in despair and hopelessness, and concentrate on a few basic questions to keep the process focused. You'll get the idea from the demonstration, but I'll write those questions down to help us remember them.' At the bottom of the sheet I write:

— What do you want?
— How can you get it?
— What help do you need?

— Can you do that?

Anna and I sit on the cushions and I ask everybody else to move so they can see Anna and give her attention.

'All right, Anna. Is there anything you need to do before we start? Yawn, scream, shake, cry?' Anna takes the opportunity to stretch her back and shake her arms. I take her hands and give her my full attention.

'Great. Now, don't think too hard and answer quickly. Keep moving. Ready?'

'Yes.'

'What do you want, Anna?'

'Peace and quiet.'

'What else do you want?'

'To be happy.'

'What else?'

'For life to be easy.'

'What else do you want?'

'To deal with Tony.'

'What else?'

'To finish papering the kitchen.'

'What else?'

'To make friends.'

'What else do you want, Anna?'

'To sort things out with my mother.'

We stay with 'What do you want?' for several more minutes, until Anna has put together a list of things she wants, mostly for herself, some for other people and for people in general.

'Is there one of the things you want that's particularly important?' I ask.

'To sort things out with Tony, I suppose,' says Anna.

'Okay. How can you do that?'

Anna pauses. 'I don't know.'

'Hello pattern,' I say. The pattern doesn't like it, and Anna laughs to clear the block. 'What can you do about Tony?'

'I could talk to him.'

'Could you?'

'No. He wouldn't listen.'

'What else could you do?'

'I could tell him I was leaving.'

'Could you?'

Anna shivers. 'Yes.'

'When?'

'Oh. Soon.'

'This week?'

Anna laughs. 'No. The following week.'

'So by a week on Friday you'll have told Tony you're leaving.'

'Oh god. Yes.'

'Do you need any help to do that?'

'Some counselling?'

'Where will you get that?'

'Margaret, perhaps.'

'Can you organize that?'

'Yes, I expect so.'

'When will you organize it?'

'Straight after this session.'

'Anything else you need to follow through on the Tony decision?'

'A new job.'

'How can you get that?'

'Look for one.'

'Where?'

'Oh god. In the *Law Society Gazette*. I'll ask around.'

'Who will you ask?'

'Um. Frances at Livingston McNulty. David Carruthers.'

'When?'

'Oh, Frances tomorrow lunchtime. I'll ring David tomorrow afternoon if Tony isn't in the office.'

Ten minutes later Anna has made so many decisions about her life that she has a problem recalling them all, but they're all realistic, all feasible, and having made them has lifted a great weight of indecision and helplessness off her shoulders. While she takes a few minutes to write down all the decisions she has made everybody else has a short break.

'There,' she says. 'Twenty-three decisions in fifteen minutes. I think what I'll do is pin the list up and tick things off as I do them.'

'Sounds good,' I say, 'but remember that you can always change your mind. Why don't you write and tell me when you've dealt with them all?'

'Okay. I will. You wait.'

By the time everybody comes back I've put the playing cards out again, twelve this time, face down. Surely this will defeat Paul, I think meanly.

We sit in a circle round the cards and I explain that we shall do the same exercise in pairs, taking ten minutes each, twenty minutes altogether. I suggest that they have a paper and pen ready in case there's anything they need to write down, and remind them briefly that the purpose of the exercise is to support somebody while they make decisions, not to advise, not to listen to their life stories, and not to console and sympathize.

When they choose their cards I watch Paul very deliberately hold back until there is one card left, and when both he and I realize that his partner is David we look at each other and smile knowingly.

Each pair finds a comfortable place on the floor and settles down to twenty minutes of creative decision-making. I put more wood on the fire and listen to the process. I can hear Sarah deciding to tell Jim how she feels about their relationship. 'When?' asks Judith. 'I don't know, I don't know. On Wednesday.' David is supporting Paul, who is talking very fast, trying to get as many decisions as possible into the available time, rather like *Mastermind*.

After ten minutes they change roles, and after another ten minutes we come together again in the circle.

Once round the circle for a word to describe each person's feelings: clear, bright, stunned, amazing, exhausted, great, wonderful, tired, clear, good, very aware. 'Drained,' says Paul.

'Before we play a game and use our bodies again, I'd like to hear one decision that each person has taken, one direction that each of you wants your life to go in. Who's going to start?'

'In the next week,' says Ursula, 'I'm going to talk with Wolfgang for at least an hour about sharing the housework more equally.'

'Well,' says Ray, 'I'm going to put adverts in six shop windows about doing carpentry work.'

'I'm going to tell Tony I'm leaving,' says Anna, 'and I'm going to start an evening class in self-defence.'

Penny laughs. 'I'm going to do a class too, in creative writing. I'm going to register tomorrow.'

'I'm not going to do the Paris trip next term,' says Glenys. 'I'll tell them this week.'

'Mine's a bit feeble,' says Margaret. 'I'm going to smile at three people every day for a fortnight.'

'What's feeble about that?' asks David. 'I'm going to tell everybody in the house I live in how much I appreciate them.'

'I'm going to give a talk to my church group on Thursday about unconditional love,' says Wolfgang.

'I'm going to find out if there's a men's counselling group in Cambridge,' says Paul, 'and join it.'

'I'm going to get Jim to sit down so I can tell him how I feel about our relationship and how I want it to be for me and Amy,' says Sarah.

'I think I'm going to write an article about love and feminism for our women's newsletter,' says Judith. Judith the sceptic.

'And I shall write to my father,' says Maurice. 'I'll write tomorrow and tell him all about what's happening in my life, in a way he'll be able to understand. I shall re-establish communication.'

'It all sounds wonderful,' I say. 'Everybody taking their life in their own hands and being willing to take risks. This is the way the world will change. Let's play a game where we have to take a risk, a leap of faith in ourselves. It's called "Trust Fall".'

It's watches and jewellery off again, and twelve of us range ourselves in two lines of six, facing each other a couple of feet apart. Each of us puts our arms out in front of us, hands palm-upwards. The thirteenth person — it's me first, to prove that it works — stands on a chair, the highest we can find, at one end of the double row. When I say I'm ready I fall, like a felled tree, into the arms of my twelve new friends, where I lie while they rock me for a few seconds.

'I'm surprised it's so easy to take the weight,' says Penny.

'It's because there are so many of us,' replies Ray.

Chapter Eleven

Demanding the Impossible

If I don't stop it, the mid-afternoon break will go on for ever while people plan their futures. Is that a feeling or a fact? Whichever it is, I go through to the kitchen and round them up.

Last session of the day, last session of the weekend, and anything could happen. I explain the game we're going to play.

We are all hums, little blind cave-dwelling animals who find each other by perpetually humming. But sadly, one of us has lost their hum, and doesn't know where to find it. The rest of us must find the humless one and show our love and compassion by holding on to poor humless and stopping humming for a while.

We all go on hands and knees, the hums' usual method of locomotion, and shut our eyes. I crawl over to an invisible hum and whisper in its ear, 'You're the humless,' then say to everybody, 'All except the humless start humming, and keep humming until you find humless. Then stop humming.'

Now all we have to do is find the humless. Twelve hums and one humless, crawling round the floor with our eyes closed. 'Mmmmmm?' 'Mmmmmmmmmm.' 'Mmmmmmmmm?' 'Mmm!' 'Mmmm? . . . mmm . . . ah.' As hums find the humless and stop humming, the noise level diminishes, until there is only one voice, plaintively calling. 'Mmm? Mmmmmmmmmmmm . . . where are you all?'

We open our eyes to see Glenys crawling round behind the chairs under the window, at the other end of the room from the massed humless. She laughs and crawls rapidly across the room, and we all collapse in giggles round the fire.

'I want to talk about impossible things,' I say. 'We've seen how patterns and blocks come up with a theme song of helplessness: "I can't, I can't, I can't." When many people's patterns interlock, we end up with groups of people, whole societies, saying, "We can't, we can't. It can't be done. It can't be changed. It's impossible." But just because a whole society is going round in a depressed state of helplessness, saying "We can't", it still doesn't mean that we should support those feelings of helplessness. Feelings are to be felt, and even when it's a feeling shared by a lot of people, the situation both for the individuals and for the group can only be improved by allowing everybody to express their feelings in a safe and supported way.

' "Demanding the impossible" has been a catch-phrase of the women's movement for a long time, and by it women mean demanding, for instance, that all human beings are treated as equals, and that male violence is stopped, things which most people in our society believe to be impossible.

'From the point of view of the world we've been exploring this weekend, the world of unconditional love, many apparently impossible things become believable. They *feel* difficult to believe, because we are not used to seeing things in this light, but I'd like to try a few ideas out and see how we react to them. Maurice, could you bring that sheet of paper that's pinned to the blackboard?'

On the back of the sheet I've written out:

Eleven 'impossible' beliefs

— Unconditional love is not only a theoretical possibility; it can be achieved in reality. Unconditional love works, individually, socially and politically.
— Everybody can be responsible for anything. There is no limit to what we can be responsible for.
— Everybody loves everybody whether they acknowledge it or not.
— There is no limit to love between people.
— There is no limit to the number of people we can acknowledge our love towards, and no limit to the ways in which we can express our love.
— Once the love between two people has been acknowledged, it can never be rationally denied.
— When all the circumstances are taken into account, everybody

always does their best to act lovingly and intelligently.
— Blame is the most useless thing in the world.
— However bad things seem, feeling our feelings *always* makes things better.
— Nobody ever voluntarily puts themself in a situation which they can't handle.
— A complete faith in love and intelligence will *always* find a solution to satisfy everybody's rational needs.

'I'll say something about each of these beliefs as we come to them, but this is a group exercise, so don't let me do all the talking.

'The first is a belief that love — the flow of intelligence and creativity — really *does* work. It's the belief that takes feelings of helplessness into account, but constantly affirms our individual power to act and change.'

'Hmmm. It's maybe true,' says Anna, 'but it's such hard work constantly dealing with things, constantly battling against other people's negativity and despair. Surely we have to think about how much we can handle, how much we can take on.'

'Well, yes,' says Margaret, 'but isn't it harder work *not* to deal with things, at least in our own lives? When I made all those decisions earlier on, when I *did* deal with things, I felt so much better.'

Anna nods. 'Yes, but that's only for yourself. Take Tony, for instance. I'd have to take *hours* to deal with things with him, talking to him, counselling on the feelings. It's much easier not to deal with it. And as for people in general . . .'

'. . . you just give up?' I add.

Anna smiles. 'I just give up?' she asks. 'No. I don't give up. But it's not the right time now. Hang on.' She pauses. 'I choose not to deal with that now. Okay? It's not that I can't deal with it, because I can. It's not that Tony couldn't deal with it if he chose to, but he probably doesn't choose to. That's not my problem. Is it?'

'All very interesting,' I say. 'Do you want my thoughts on the subject?'

'Of course we do,' says Margaret, then hesitates. 'Of course I do.'

'Well, I think we *can* deal with anything, including seemingly impossible things like world peace and international violence, but we can also choose, like Anna, not to deal with things at present. And only *we* know what we can handle without becoming overwhelmed or reminded too much of our own pain, so we mustn't let ourselves be bullied into dealing with things we choose not to deal with. My other thought is that Margaret is right when she says that unrestrained love makes life easier. It certainly does in the long run, as we deal with the backlog of blocks and patterns. It's sometimes difficult when we're in mid-process, and everything *seems* awful, to believe that the practice of unconditional love really does make life easier and the world better. But it does. Love works.

'Responsibility next. This comes from a talk by Harvey Jackins called "Who's in Charge?". He says, "Each human being is in full charge of the entire universe . . . There is no limit to what a human being can be responsible for." To me this involves intelligence and sensitivity, reacting appropriately to our surroundings all the time.'

'But you can't be responsible for *everything*,' says Ray. 'It's impossible. I can only just be responsible for myself.'

'That's a good start,' I say. 'But I didn't say *everything*, even though I think — do I? — that that's true. I said *anything*. The way Harvey Jackins puts it is that we are either responsible or not; we can't be in-between, and since we *are* responsible, there's no logical limit to what we can be responsible for.'

'It's a question of the alternatives again,' says David. 'The alternative belief is that we can't help what happens in the world, which just isn't true. If people starve in Mozambique of course it's my responsibility. I helped cause it. I can do something about it.'

'Contradicting helplessness again,' says Anna.

'One more point about responsibility,' I say. 'Because we are highly intelligent and very responsible doesn't necessarily mean that we can do everything we want to. We don't always have the resources — the time, the money, the energy. We need to remember how important *we* are, and put ourselves first. Altruism is all very well, but it's not far from martyrdom, and we are part of our responsibility too.'

'And presumably,' says Glenys, 'when we do take responsibility and act intelligently, we realize there's enough time and enough resources in the world to fulfil everybody's needs, including our own.'

'An almost impossible belief,' adds Judith.

The third 'impossible' belief: everybody loves everybody. 'The natural relationship between any two human beings is loving affection, communication and co-operation.'

'Even Tony,' says Anna.

'Even Jane,' says Sarah.

'Even if you don't know them?' asks Ursula.

'Ronald Reagan?' David shudders.

'What's the alternative?' I ask.

'I heard recently about this scheme for Americans to write to Russians they don't know,' says Maurice. 'They send a photograph of themselves, perhaps their children too, and talk about themselves and how they feel about peace and co-operation. That's loving someone you don't know.'

'Loving your enemy,' says Judith.

'You have to,' says Wolfgang.

'Which brings us to the fourth and fifth "impossible" beliefs,' I say. 'No limits.'

'We could talk about this for weeks,' says Paul. 'No limit to the number of people you can love? I have a lot of problems with that. Multiple relationships, promiscuity.'

'Is that what it means?' asks Glenys, looking slightly alarmed.

Nobody answers for a few seconds. I poke the fire.

'Yes,' says David 'I think it does, but it means rethinking all our assumptions about what loving people means. I don't think we have much idea about what intelligent and sensitive closeness between people could be like. It's *so* blocked and *so* patterned. We'd need to rethink everything about relationships and couples and marriage and families and parenting and sex. Especially sex. Phew, that really *does* seem impossible.'

'Can it be done?' I ask.

Another long silence, during which the flames break through where I was poking.

'What's the alternative?' asks Penny. Everyone laughs.

'Number six,' I say. 'Once you've loved somebody, you always love them. What a lot of distress this one contradicts. How do we usually "end" relationships — splitting up, breaking up, divorce, separation, good riddance?'

'I've never believed in that,' says Penny. 'I still know everybody I've ever had a relationship with, from the last ten years, anyway. I still see them, keep in touch. Yes, I love them and they love me.'

'It's sad,' says Anna. 'We're singing this song in the choir about a woman who kills her husband so she can marry someone else. Then on her wedding day a dove reminds her so much of her guilt that she goes and drowns herself. The husband may have been a bastard, of course, but it's ridiculous that someone should think they have to kill one person they love in order to love another.'

'It's not love, is it?' says Paul. 'It's sex. You can *love* who you want, but you can't have sex with them.'

'But that's what David was saying,' says Penny. 'We don't have much idea of what closeness is like when it's not patterned. You know, I don't *really* know what sex is. That's not true; I do, but either it's part of real loving or it's part of oppression.' She pauses. 'If it's part of real loving I think you can be physically close to as many people as you choose to be. The problem is that it almost never is. It's too patterned, too oppressive. Mmmm.'

'I don't understand,' says Paul. 'How about getting together later to talk about it?'

'We'll see,' says Penny.

'Okay,' I say. 'Slight change of tack next, so let's take a minute to stretch and shake before we go on.'

Margaret crawls over to me and hugs me. 'I do love you,' she says, running her fingers through my hair. 'I like that,' I say, grinning.

'Everybody always does their best,' I say when everybody has finished yawning and groaning. 'When we act out of pain and distress we do it because we're patterned to do it, not because that's the way we are. We can always do better, but we always do our best to act intelligently all the time. Even when we are behaving oppressively or insensitively we are doing our best; even when we fail or are wrong we are doing our best. A difficult belief to come to terms with.'

'Even Reagan?' asks David again.

'Even Margaret Thatcher?' asks Judith. 'Oh god. Sometimes the unconditional love goes too far.'

'I think that's her problem,' says Ray. 'Nobody loves her, and she doesn't have anyone to love. If somebody gave her a hug she'd probably explode.'

Penny laughs. 'Sorry,' she says, 'I just had this picture of Tammy hugging Margaret Thatcher. She'd hug anyone. It's amazing how much we can learn from children, and it's so sad that we train it out of them. A complete faith in human nature, that's what she has.'

'Blame,' I go on. 'We all do our best all the time and so does everybody else, so neither we nor anybody else deserves to be blamed. Blame is total invalidation and denies responsibility. Blame is negative and counter-productive, a real block. And now I feel quite angry.' I stop to shake my hands vigorously.

Nobody says anything. Perhaps they're frightened of my anger; perhaps we did enough about blame yesterday; perhaps they don't like me.

'Well felt,' says Maurice. 'Ten out of ten. You've demonstrated the next point really well.'

I laugh. 'Thank you, Maurice. I think we've probably covered it already, but I do think this one's vitally important. I've heard so many people say to me things like, "I don't want to get into that, it's too heavy," or, "I just get bogged down in my feelings." I want to shake them and shout, "No, the heaviness is a feeling; feel it and it will go"; "You're not bogged down in your feelings, you're bogged down because you're *not* feeling your feelings." Okay, so there are lots of times when it's not appropriate to feel the feelings, and we can choose when to deal with them, but if we're serious about dealing with the blocks to our true loving nature we have to feel those feelings. And when we do, things can only get better. Deep pain and distress may take a long time to deal with, of course, though not always. The patterns will say, "Oh, this is awful and things are getting worse and worse. You might as well stop all this feeling and go away and leave me alone." But that's the pattern talking, not the person. It's not true that it only gets worse. Feeling feelings *always* makes things better. For everyone.

' "Impossible" belief number ten.'

'Seems obvious to me,' says David. 'It's the "voluntarily" that's important, because the pressures can be very subtle.'

'How does this fit in with choosing not to handle something?' asks Sarah.

'Isn't it the difference between "a situation they can't handle" and "a situation they choose not to handle",' says Penny, 'the difference between helplessness and choice?'

'And it's about making people do things they don't want to by taking power over them,' says Judith. 'The trouble is that people are so rarely in situations they've actively chosen to be in. Back to the question of choice again.'

'Okay. The last one. There's always a solution to satisfy everyone.'

'Difficult to believe,' says Wolfgang, 'because it so rarely happens. If I get what I want you won't get what you want.'

'Isn't that assuming that getting it is the only answer that will satisfy you both?' asks Sarah.

Wolfgang stops to think. 'Hmm. I like that. And we could share it, whatever it is.'

'But what's wrong,' says Judith, 'is that it's always the same people who *don't* get it and the same people who *don't* share it. It's all very well giving something up and saying that's okay, but it's much easier for it to be okay if you're not always giving things up.'

'I don't understand,' says Ursula.

'Well, start where Wolfgang started — if I get what I want you won't get what you want. That suggests that there isn't enough of whatever it is to go round — could be anything, food, housing, time, attention. But the biggest reason why there isn't enough to go round is that some people are taking far more than they rationally need. Rationally — yes, well, that's a debatable point, but I'll accept it for now. Taking more than you rationally need is taking advantage of privilege, being greedy. And it's quite easy to give little things up if you've got enough — like if a childless man says, "Yes, I'll give up some of my time to run a crèche." But if a single mother says the same thing, she's giving up something she doesn't have, free time without children in this case. Money's another one — it's easy enough to sponsor Save the Children if you've got plenty of spare cash, *and* you'll get the kudos for being a good benefactor, but someone on social security might believe passionately in their responsibility towards Third-World kids and not be able to give anything.'

'So what are you saying about finding solutions?' asks Ursula.

Judith laughs. 'You're right,' she says. 'And so am I. There are solutions, and we can act, *and* being rational means recognizing inequality of circumstances. But yes, I *do* believe that a complete faith in love and intelligence will always find solutions to satisfy everybody's rational needs.'

'Thank you everybody,' I say. 'I'd like to move on now, with a slight change of emphasis.

'When we were talking about responsibility, I said that our resources are limited, and one of the resources which is limited is time. Time's a tricky concept, because although it's limited, it's usually nothing like as limited as we feel it is. I think it's a mistake to think that there isn't time to do everything we want to do. Just because we don't have time to do everything now, it doesn't mean that the opportunity will never arise again. As Tom Robbins writes at the end of his novel *Still Life with Woodpecker*, "It's never too late to have a happy childhood." Just because something happens once, it doesn't mean that something similar and equally good won't happen again. "If a thing has happened once, it will surely happen again," says the I *Ching*. And just because a particular event is only going to happen once, it doesn't mean that we can't try out in advance the different ways we might do it.

'We've got another hour together, and then we'll be saying goodbye to each other. That hour is only an hour, and we can't turn it into two hours whatever we do. Even if we stay on afterwards, we'll have to leave each other eventually. But we can get some idea of how the parting will go by trying it out in a few different ways now. I've chosen saying goodbye because it's surrounded by painful memories for most people — letting friends go, rejection, things unsaid, loss.

'I've said enough. Let's do it. Choose somebody now that it's going to be difficult to say goodbye to at the end of the workshop.'

It takes a few minutes for people to choose their partners, and it's interesting to see who chooses who. Paul and Ursula are together again, Judith and Anna, Margaret and David, Sarah and Wolfgang, and Penny moves over beside Ray.

'Right. Here's the setting. It's late in the evening and you've been having a wonderful time together — a meal and then a long talk, a real closeness. But now it's time to go. You'll need to decide which of you is leaving, and start to say goodbye. You know that there's no desperate hurry, but it's a long journey home. See how long it takes to say goodbye, how you do it, how it feels. Off you go.'

I watch the handholding, the hugging, the long looks into each other's eyes, the 'see you again soon', the 'I wish you didn't have to go yet'. David shakes, Ursula cries. Judith and Anna have parted and join me by the fire, so have Ray and Penny. Wolfgang hugs Sarah like a bear. 'You'd better go now,' says Sarah, half smiling, half pushing him away. 'Goodnight,' says Wolfgang and backs through the imaginary door. David and Margaret hug and part,

Ursula and Paul are still locked in a fond embrace.

'Are you staying the night?' asks Wolfgang.

Paul and Ursula look up; Paul smiles wryly and Ursula blushes. Wolfgang goes over to them and puts his arms round them both. The three of them hug and we move on.

'Parting number two. The other person in the pair is leaving this time. Can you all stand up and face each other about three feet apart? Good. The one that's leaving is on a boat and you're saying goodbye over the rail. You've just had a wonderful holiday together, and you won't see each other for several months. It's two minutes before the boat leaves. Time to say goodbye.'

Hugging over imaginary rails, 'send me a postcard', 'have a good trip'. A much lighter feel in the air. 'Oooooooooooo' — my imitation of a ship's horn. 'The boat's leaving.' 'Cheerio.' 'See you.' 'I love you.'

The third and last departure. 'Back to the first person leaving. An airport terminal this time. Final call any minute. Just time for a final farewell after a fantastic week together. Hurry.'

Fast and furious hugging between David and Margaret; a lot of people just spending half a minute in silent mutual appreciation.

'Last call for Flight BA177,' I call. 'Will the remaining passengers for Flight BA177 report now to passport control?'

Quick last kisses and the parting is over. Everybody breathes again.

'Well done. Now take a couple of minutes with your partner to talk about those different partings, what was going on, how you were feeling, maybe decide which you found the easiest.'

While they talk I lie down on my back on the hearthrug and shut my eyes, feel the warmth from the fire. I could easily fall asleep.

'Right. Back into a circle when you're ready. Nearly there now. Does anybody need to do or say anything before we go on?'

Margaret sighs. 'I'm just feeling really high,' she says. 'Spaced out almost, but no, I'm really here too. I feel like . . . like anything could happen and it would be all right. That's what it is. I feel so safe in this group. At home.' She breathes out deeply.

'Thank you, Margaret.' I smile at her. 'I want to teach you all another Sufi song.' The words are:

I love you whether I know it or not,
I love you whether I show it or not;

There are so many things I haven't said inside my heart,
Perhaps now is a good time to start.

We sing it through several times until everybody has the words.
Then we start to move round the room, and every time we sing
it to a different person, taking their hands and looking lovingly
at them, before moving on. I stop singing when I've made the
connection with each of the other people, but nobody else seems
to want to stop. It's only when I drop out and stand meaningfully
by the fire that the singing gradually dies away.

Without needing to say anything we join hands in a circle. 'Who'd
like to be the centre of attention for a few minutes,' I ask. 'How
about you, Margaret?'

Margaret nods enthusiastically.

'Good. Then let go of David's hand and move into the centre
of the circle keeping hold of Sarah's hand. Everybody else keep
holding hands on both sides, except you, David. You'll be leading
our spiral. Now let's all sing "Heart to heart" while we move slowly
in a spiral round Margaret, wrapping her in love. You keep
absolutely still, Margaret; just feel the warmth surrounding you.
Is everybody clear about what we're doing?'

We all move slowly round Margaret in a smaller and smaller spiral
as she is wrapped up in the arms of the other people in the group,
and we sing as we walk: Heart to heart, mind to mind, body to
body; it's a love divine. Sarah and Anna start to harmonize, and
then we just hum the tune as David, last in the line, wraps himself
round everybody else.

'Let's imagine we're one organism,' I say from somewhere inside
the hug. 'Listen to each other's breathing, and gradually all start
to breathe together.' I look round as much as I can with my chin
on Ray's shoulder and my forehead against Judith's. Everybody
has their eyes shut, breathing deeply, breathing together. I close
my eyes and turn my head; my cheek brushes against Judith's.
Breathing, breathing. Somebody starts crying quietly — Margaret.
'I'm fine,' she sobs. 'It's great. I'm enjoying myself so much.'

'Can you get us out of this again, Margaret? Duck under
everybody's arms and get to the outside, but keep hold of hands
until we're back in the circle.'

The spiral organism empties from the inside out, and once again
we stand holding hands in a circle.

'Take a minute to make contact with each of the other people in the group,' I say. 'Remember the connections you've made this weekend, that once you've acknowledged the love between you, you can never rationally deny it.'

Margaret continues to cry as she smiles at everybody. Paul smiles at David for a long time. I feel very tired.

'Let's take all the love and healing we've experienced in the group and remember that we can change the world through love. We'll turn outwards now and sing three oms for the healing of the earth.'

We all turn and face outwards, hold hands again.

The open sound of the first om spreads outwards from our small group. The second om follows. The third is picked up again and again, high, low, harmonized, the original note picked up again. Eventually the sound fades. We stand silent, hand in hand.

'And now?' asks Paul.

Although that's the end of our weekend together, it takes a long time for people to leave. We make a list of names and addresses so we can stay in touch. I promise to write to everybody and send them a copy of everything that's been written down.

'How are *you* feeling?' asks David.

'Me? Oh, I'm very tired,' I say. 'I think it's because giving constant attention is physically tiring. I always feel worn out at the end of a weekend, but I expect I'll wake up after a good meal.'

'I really enjoyed it,' says David. 'I'm amazed how much we've done in two days.'

Tamsin runs through from the hall. 'Hello, John. Guess what?'

'Don't know until you tell me.'

'We went to some gardens with a pond and lots and *lots* of rhododendrons. And guess what?'

'Mmm?'

'We played meditations, me and Saul and Catherine.'

'How was that?'

'Oh, I won.'

★   ★   ★

When I got home I typed out the address list, the group statement on love from the meditation, the words of the chants, the counselling 'do's' and 'don'ts', the directions from the choice exercise and the eleven 'impossible' things. Then I wrote the covering letter:

Laurieston, October 30th

Dear friends,

Thank you so much for helping to create such an inspiring workshop. I enjoyed being with you all very much, and learnt a great deal from you — I hope you learnt something too.

I'm enclosing with this letter all the bits and pieces I said I would.

If you have the time and inclination to write, I'd love to hear your thoughts and feelings about how the weekend was for you — the things that were good, the things that could have been better. And I'd like to hear what's happening in your life, too, your challenges, your hopes, your successes. I promise you'll get a reply.

Lots of love and hugs,

John

In the next month or so I heard from Margaret, Maurice, Anna and Sarah.

Sarah wrote: 'I've been writing to you in my thoughts often, but getting it down on paper has taken some time. Every time I think back to our weekend together I feel renourished. The sincerity was overwhelming. When I got home Jim was waiting up for me, calm and relaxed. We talked for at least two hours after Amy was in bed, and when he heard everything I had to say he told me it had really touched him too.

'I've been a bit low in the last week or so, a faraway feeling, doubt and irritation. I shouted at Jim again yesterday — got a sore throat. But I know what I *want* now. My own space, Jim to take his share of Amy. And I've sorted out my job, to do it at home. I asked for a phone, and John (the publisher I work for) said, "How sensible." "Of course," I said. "I am."'

Maurice wrote on a postcard which said, 'Too much of a good thing can be wonderful — Mae West'; 'Wow. It *does* work. I still feel very vulnerable, too open (is that possible . . .) — how do you deal with that? I get hurt when I'm too vulnerable, or perhaps I'm not expressing the feelings enough. Working at it. Had a really good reply from my father. He said "I never thought we'd be able to say things like this to each other." Thank you, thank you.'

And now it's nearly six months since we all met in that warm room for our October love weekend; I'm going back to the same place to lead another group in three weeks' time. Another group, more love.

This morning I had a letter from Penny and a card with pressed rhododendrons on from Tamsin. At the end of her letter Penny writes: 'Another thing I wanted to tell you. Remember Ray? I bumped into him in the Holloway Road a couple of days ago, he's doing a training scheme in Islington. We went to have tea together, and got into talking about *the* weekend. He said it seemed to have a very long-lasting effect on him. He said he'd been to see the woman he split up with just before the workshop, and he could see what had been going on between them without getting caught up in it all again. Then he started this course in north London where he didn't know anybody. And he said that since he had experienced so many open, loving people in the workshop who accepted him just as he is, he could relax in the new place and trust that he'd find good people to be with, and let things happen instead of frantically grasping for allies. And sure enough there were some good people at the college, and they got together . . .

'I thought you'd like to hear that. A bit late for feedback, but it'll maybe give you an extra bit of energy for the book.

'Strength, love, happiness, patience, satisfaction, excitement and energy — and a warm hug. Penny.'

Techniques Used in the Workshop

Over the years I have learnt many different techniques and exercises that can be used in groups. I don't use just one; I use whatever works. At the same time I do find some techniques work better for me than others, and the four that I make the most use of are co-counselling, psychosynthesis, Reichian bodywork and new games.

Much of the workshop is based on the theory and practice of co-counselling, especially the branch of counselling called Re-evaluation Co-counselling. If you would like to read more about co-counselling, useful books are:

Harvey Jackins (1965) *The Human Side of Human Beings: The Theory of Re-evaluation Counselling* Rational Island Publishers, Seattle

Rose Evison and Richard Horobin (1983) *How to Change Yourself and Your World: A Manual of Co-counselling Theory and Practice* Co-counselling Phoenix, 5 Victoria Road, Sheffield

The two meditations are based on techniques from psychosynthesis, a transpersonal psychological technique evolved by a pupil of Jung's called Roberto Assagioli. The best book on psychosynthesis is called:

Piero Ferrucci (1982) *What We May Be: The Visions and Techniques of Psychosynthesis* Turnstone Press, Wellingborough

The connections between our physical body and our emotions have been explored in depth by followers of the work of Wilhelm Reich, usually called Reichian or neo-Reichian bodywork. For more information in this area, I can recommend:

Alexander Lowen (1976) *Bioenergetics* Penguin, London
David Boadella (ed.) (1976) *In the Wake of Reich* Coventure, London

I sometimes make up games myself, but most of my workshop games come from other people's collections, and especially from the work of the New Games Foundation. Books with good ideas for non-competitive games are:

New Games Foundation (1978) *The New Games Book* Sidgwick and Jackson, London
Matt Weinstein and Joel Goodman (1980) *Playfair: Everybody's Guide to Noncompetitive Play* Impact Publishers, San Luis Obispo
'For the Fun of it: Selected Cooperative Games for Children and Adults' in Stephanie Judson (1984) *A Manual on Nonviolence and Children* New Society Publishers, Philadelphia

A very good introduction to a range of techniques of self-help therapy, together with an excellent critique of the political role of therapy, is: Sheila Ernst and Lucy Goodison (1981) *In Our Own Hands: A Book of Self-Help Therapy*, The Women's Press, London. *The Reality Game: A Guide to Humanistic Counselling and Therapy* by John Rowan (1983), Routledge and Kegan Paul, London, is also a useful introduction to the theory of therapy, though to my mind it sometimes veers towards a rather mechanistic psychoanalytical approach. It contains at the end a useful list of contact addresses and telephone numbers.

If you are interested in organizing or taking part in a workshop similar to the one described in *Making Love Work*, please write to me, care of the publishers, for further information. Please enclose a stamped addressed envelope.

Books Mentioned in the Text

Bernard, Jessie (1976) *The Future of Marriage* Penguin
Bohm, David (1983) *Wholeness and the Implicate Order* Ark (Routledge and Kegan Paul)
Branden, Nathaniel (1981) *The Psychology of Romantic Love* Bantam
Campbell, Susan (1983) *Earth Community: Living Experiments in Cultural Transformation* Evolutionary Press
Collis, John Stewart (1973) *The Worm Forgives the Plough* Penguin
Dowling, Colette (1982) *The Cinderella Complex: Women's Hidden Fear of Independence* Fontana
Dworkin, Andrea (1983) 'The Politics of Intelligence' in *Right-Wing Women* The Women's Press
Firestone, Shulamith (1979) *The Dialectic of Sex: The Case for Feminist Revolution* The Women's Press (originally published 1971)
Ford, Edward E. (1983) *The Freedom to Love* Winston Press
Fromm, Erich (1975) *The Art of Loving* Unwin (originally published 1957)
Gathorne-Hardy, Jonathan (1983) *Love, Sex, Marriage and Divorce* Paladin
Goldman, Emma (1979) *Red Emma Speaks* Wildwood House
Goodison, Lucy (1983) 'Really being in love means wanting to live in a different world' in Sue Cartledge and Joanna Ryan (eds.) *Sex and Love: New Thoughts on Old Contradictions* The Women's Press
Greer, Germaine (1981) *The Female Eunuch* Granada (originally published 1970)
Helmbold, Lois Rita and Amber Hollibaugh (1982) 'The family: what holds us, what hurts us' in Steve Rosskamm Shalom (ed.) *Socialist Visions* Pluto Press

Hoffmann, David (1983) *The Holistic Herbal* Findhorn Press

Jackins, Harvey (1973) *The Human Situation* Rational Island Publishers

Jennings, Paula (1981) Letter to WIRES, reprinted in *Love Your Enemy?: The Debate Between Heterosexual Feminism and Political Lesbianism* Onlywomen Press

Johnston, William (1981) *The Inner Eye of Love: Mysticism and Religion* Collins (Fount)

Keyes, Ken (1979) A *Conscious Person's Guide to Relationships* Living Love Publications

Lao Tze (1969) *Tao Te Ching* Penguin

Leland, Stephanie (1983) 'Feminism and ecology: theoretical connections' in Leonie Caldicott and Stephanie Leland (eds.) *Reclaim the Earth: Women Speak Out for Life on Earth* The Women's Press

Lewis, C. S. (1963) *The Four Loves* Collins (Fount)

Lovelock, John (1982) *Gaia: A New Look at Life on Earth* Oxford University Press

Merton, Thomas (1979) *Love and Living* Sheldon Press

Ray, Sondra (1976) *I Deserve Love* Celestial Arts

Ray, Sondra (1977) *Loving Relationships* Celestial Arts

Sarsby, Jacqueline (1983) *Romantic Love and Society: Its Place in the Modern World* Penguin

Sartre, Jean-Paul (1969) *Being and Nothingness* Methuen

Schutz, William C. (1973) *Joy: Expanding Human Awareness* Penguin

Tweedie, Jill (1980) *In the Name of Love* Granada

Vannoy, Russell (1980) *Sex Without Love: A Philosophical Exploration* Prometheus Books

Watts, Alan (1979) *Tao: The Watercourse Way* Penguin